THE GREATEST GANGSTER MOVIE YOU'VE NEVER SEEN:

Abel Ferrara's The Funeral

By Danny Stewart

First Edition, 2023
BearManor Media
ISBN: 979-8-88771-697-8

Published in the USA by Bear Manor Media

Dedicated to Ken Kelsch & Sian Sophie Stewart

Ken Kelsch: Father, cinematographer, teacher, and Vietnam veteran.

(July 8, 1947 – December 11, 2023)

Sian Sophie Stewart: Daughter, mother, sister, and singer.

(August 5, 1990 – July 14, 2024)

Contents

Introduction:
THE GREATEST GANGSTER MOVIE YOU'VE NEVER SEEN:
Abel Ferrara's The Funeral

In the dimly lit alleys of the gangster genre, there exists a realm of shadows and intrigue where morality is murky, and power reigns supreme. It is within this captivating world that we embark on a journey, guided by the cinematic prowess of visionary director Abel Ferrara and his landmark film, "The Funeral." Through the lens of this gritty and atmospheric masterpiece, we delve deep into the heart of organized crime, exploring its dark complexities and timeless themes. "The Funeral" stands as an overlooked cornerstone of the gangster genre, a film that transcends its narrative confines to offer a profound meditation on family, loyalty, and the human condition. Set against the backdrop of 1930s New York City, the film follows the tumultuous journey of the Tempio brothers as they navigate the treacherous waters of organized crime and personal tragedy. With its richly developed characters, haunting imagery, and thematic depth, "The Funeral" serves as the perfect entry point for our exploration of the gangster genre and the themes that define it. But my journey does not end with "The Funeral." In these pages venture further into the cinematic universe of Abel Ferrara, uncovering the hidden gems and profound insights that await us. Through in-depth interviews with filmmaker Abel Ferrara, director of photography Ken Kelsch, production designer Charlie M. Lagola, costume designer Mindy Eshelman, and producer Mary Kane we will gain a deeper understanding of the creative process behind Ferrara's films and the meticulous attention to detail that brings his vision to life. From the gritty streets of "Bad Lieutenant" to the existential despair of "The

Addiction," Ferrara's films serve as windows into the human soul, revealing the darkness and complexity that lurk within us all. Through the exploration of his work, you will uncover the timeless themes and universal truths that have made Ferrara one of the most influential voices in cinema. Join me as we journey into the heart of the gangster genre, guided by the masterful hand of Abel Ferrara and his unforgettable film, "The Funeral." I unravel the mysteries of organized crime and discover the hidden depths of human nature that lie beneath the surface. Welcome to the world of shadows, where truth is elusive, and danger lurks around every corner.

Author Danny Stewart: This book meant a great deal to him and is dedicated to his sister, Sian Stewart, and Ken Kelsch, who are constantly watching over him. They had a profound effect on his life and creative process. Their spirits are the wind at his back, urging him to keep moving forward.

Chapter 1

Abel Ferrara: The King in New York Filmmaking

Abel Ferrara in Sintra at Lisbon Film Festival 2017. Photo Credit: Ilya Mauter.[i]

Abel Ferrara, a renowned filmmaker from the United States, has established a strong reputation for himself with his daring and controversial films. With a dedicated focus on independent filmmaking, Ferrara has directed over 20 feature films. His notable works frequently revolve around gritty crime thrillers set in the bustling metropolis of New York. Some of the films he has directed include "9 Lives of a Wet Pussy" (1976), "The Driller Killer" (1979), "Ms. 45" (1981), "Fear City" (1984), "The Gladiator" (1986), "China Girl" (1987), "The Loner" (1988), "Cat Chaser" (1989), "King of New York" (1990), "Bad Lieutenant" (1992), "Body Snatchers" (1993), "Dangerous Game" (1993), "The Addiction" (1995), "The Funeral" (1996), "The Blackout" (1997), "New Rose

Hotel" (1998), "'R Xmas" (2001), "Mary" (2005), "Go Go Tales" (2007), "Chelsea on the Rocks" (2008), "Napoli, Napoli, Napoli" (2009), "4:44 Last Day on Earth" (2011), "Welcome to New York" (2014), "Pasolini" (2014), "Piazza Vittorio" (2017), "Alive in France" (2017), "The Projectionist" (2019), "Tommaso" (2019), "Siberia" (2020), "Sportin' Life" (2020), "Zeros and Ones" (2021), and "Padre Pio" (2022). These films delve deeply into the realm of urban violence while also exploring profound spiritual and existential themes.

Abel Ferrara is considered one of the most daring and provocative filmmakers of his generation, known for his uncompromising approach to storytelling, visceral style, and exploration of taboo subjects. Throughout his prolific career, Ferrara has tackled a wide range of themes and genres, earning both critical acclaim and controversy.

Ferrara's films often explore the darker aspects of human nature, delving into themes such as guilt, redemption, addiction, and the search for meaning in a morally ambiguous world. From his early exploitation films like "The Driller Killer" to his gritty crime dramas like "King of New York" and "Bad Lieutenant," Ferrara has demonstrated a penchant for confronting uncomfortable truths and pushing artistic boundaries. His films are characterized by their raw authenticity, provocative subject matter, and unflinching portrayal of violence and depravity.

One of the recurring themes in Ferrara's work is the exploration of moral ambiguity and the complexities of the human psyche. In films like "Bad Lieutenant" and "The Funeral," Ferrara presents morally flawed protagonists who grapple with their own demons and struggle to find redemption in a world devoid of morality. These characters are often depicted as antiheroes, navigating the murky waters of crime and corruption while wrestling with their own inner demons. Ferrara's exploration of moral ambiguity challenges traditional notions of heroism and villainy, forcing audiences to confront uncomfortable truths about human nature.

Ferrara's films frequently examine the intersection of religion, spirituality, and existential angst. Whether it's through the lens of Catholic guilt in "Bad Lieutenant" or the existential despair of "The Addiction," Ferrara's films often grapple with questions of faith, redemption, and the meaning of existence. Religious iconography and symbolism are recurring motifs in his work, serving as a backdrop for his characters' existential struggles and moral dilemmas.

In terms of reception, Ferrara's films have elicited a wide range of reactions from critics and audiences alike. While some have praised his bold vision and uncompromising storytelling, others have criticized his films for their graphic content and controversial subject matter. Ferrara's willingness to tackle taboo subjects and push the boundaries of conventional storytelling has made him a polarizing figure in the world of cinema. However, his work has undeniably left a lasting impact on the film industry, inspiring countless filmmakers and challenging audiences to confront uncomfortable truths about the human condition.

In addition to his thematic explorations, Ferrara's life and personal struggles have also influenced his filmmaking style. Known for his tumultuous personal life and battles with addiction, Ferrara brings a raw authenticity to his films that reflect his own experiences and world view. His films often feel like personal, cathartic expressions of his inner turmoil, with Ferrara using cinema as a means of grappling with his own demons and seeking redemption.

Abel Ferrara's body of work represents a bold and uncompromising exploration of the human condition, characterized by its raw authenticity, provocative subject matter, and unflinching portrayal of violence and depravity. Throughout his career, Ferrara has tackled a wide range of themes and genres, earning both critical acclaim and controversy. While his films may not be to everyone's taste, there's no denying the impact that Ferrara has had on the world of cinema, challenging audiences to confront uncomfortable truths about the human condition and inspiring countless filmmakers to push the boundaries of conventional storytelling.

Abel Ferrara at the Cannes Film Festival. Photo Credit: Georges Biard[ii]

Abel Ferrara. Photo Credit: Ken Kelsch.
"My existence is about making movies, so I've just got to rock and roll with the punches. You want to make movies on telephones, I'm there."– Abel Ferrara[1]

---

1 *Andrew Purcell (August 5, 2010) https://www.theguardian.com/film/2010/ aug/05/abel-ferrara-interview*

Abel Ferrara. Photo Credit: Gabriele Fuso.

Abel Ferrara. Photo Credit: Gabriele Fuso.

Abel Ferrara. Photo Credit: Gabriele Fuso.

Abel Ferrara. Photo Credit: Gabriele Fuso.

Director Abel Ferrara at the opening of the Club 57 show at MOMA, Halloween 2017. Photo Credit: Meredith Jacobson Marciano.

Fernando F. Croce on The Driller Killer: "A corruscating tale of a mind liberated by psychosis."[2]

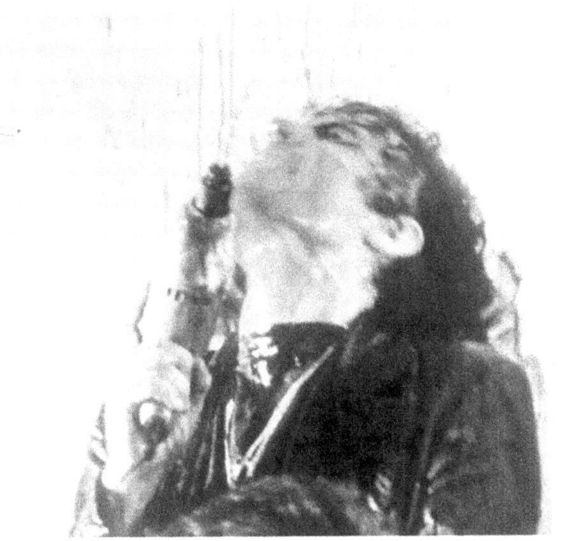

The Driller Killer (1979) Directed by Abel Ferrara. Credit: Photofest.

____

2   *https://www.cinepassion.org/Reviews/d/DrillerKiller.html*

The Driller Killer (1979) Directed by Abel Ferrara. Credit: Photofest.

This is an over-the-shoulder screenshot from the public domain film The Driller Killer, with the protagonist preparing to dispatch another victim.[iii]

This is a comparison of two screenshots from the public domain film The Driller Killer, with the protagonist playing pinball. The shots are approximately five seconds apart. This is an example of using cutting to place the viewer into the POV of the protagonist.[iv]

Chapter 2

The Dynamic Duo: Abel Ferrara and Ken Kelsch

The creative duo Abel Ferrara and Ken Kelsch. Photo Credit: Chris Kelsch.

Abel Ferrara's collaboration with director of photography Ken Kelsch has yielded some of the most visually arresting and thematically rich films of any genre, with "The Funeral" standing as a prime example of their combined talents. Released in 1996, "The

Funeral" showcases Ferrara's directorial vision and Kelsch's cinematographic prowess, resulting in a gritty and immersive portrayal of the criminal underworld. The symbiotic relationship between Ferrara and Kelsch, as well as their contributions to "The Funeral" and their collective impact on the gangster genre. Firstly, Abel Ferrara and Ken Kelsch's collaboration spans multiple films, with each project building upon the successes and innovations of the previous ones. Beginning with "The Driller Killer" in 1979, Ferrara and Kelsch established a creative partnership characterized by a shared commitment to pushing artistic boundaries and challenging audience expectations. Their collaboration continued through films such as "Bad Lieutenant," "Dangerous Game," and "The Addiction," with each project showcasing Kelsch's distinctive cinematographic style and Ferrara's uncompromising directorial vision. In "The Funeral," Ferrara and Kelsch's collaboration reaches its zenith, with Kelsch's evocative cinematography lending a haunting and atmospheric quality to the film's portrayal of the criminal underworld. Through his use of lighting, dynamic camera movements, and unconventional framing techniques, Kelsch creates a sense of foreboding and existential dread that permeates every frame of the film. The juxtaposition of shadow and light mirrors the moral ambiguity of the characters and underscores the film's exploration of themes such as guilt, redemption, and the search for meaning in a world devoid of morality. Ferrara and Kelsch's collaboration extends beyond mere aesthetics, with Kelsch's cinematography enhancing the emotional impact of the film. Through his use of close-ups and intimate framing, Kelsch allows viewers to glimpse into the inner lives of the characters, capturing the subtle nuances of their expressions and body language. This intimate approach to cinematography fosters a sense of empathy and connection with the characters, drawing audiences deeper into the emotional core of the narrative. Furthermore, Ferrara and Kelsch's collaboration in "The Funeral" exemplifies their shared commitment to authenticity and realism, with Kelsch's cinematography capturing the gritty urban landscape and the harsh realities of life in the criminal underworld. From dimly-lit back alleys to smoky jazz clubs, Kelsch's lens captures the texture and atmosphere of 1930s New York City immersing viewers in the film's historical setting. This attention to detail and historical accuracy adds depth and richness to the film's visual storytelling, enhancing its overall impact and contributing to its enduring legacy in the gangster genre.

Abel Ferrara and Ken Kelsch's collaboration in "The Funeral" represents one of the many pinnacles of their creative partnership, with Kelsch's evocative cinematography complementing Ferrara's uncompromising directorial vision to create a haunting and immersive portrayal of the criminal underworld. Their collective impact on the gangster genre cannot be overstated, with each film in their collaboration pushing artistic boundaries and challenging audience expectations. Through their shared commitment to authenticity, realism, and visual storytelling, Ferrara and Kelsch have left an indelible mark on cinema, with "The Funeral" standing as a testament to their enduring legacy as cinematic dynamos.

Ken Kelsch was a member of the ASC—the American Society of Cinematographers.

"Cinematography is a creative and interpretative process that culminates in the authorship of an original work of art rather than the simple recording of a physical event. Cinematography is not a subcategory of photography. Rather, photography is but one craft that the cinematographer uses in addition to other physical, organizational, managerial, interpretative and image-manipulating techniques to effect one coherent process."- John Hora, ASC – Definition of Cinematography, The American Cinematographer Manual[3]

---

3 *John Hora (2007). "Anamorphic Cinematography". In Burum, Stephen H. (ed.). The American Cinematographer Manual (9 ed.). ASC Press. ISBN 978-0-935578-31-7.*

Bad Lieutenant 1991 Crew at the Limelight. Photo Credit: Dennis A. Livesey.

Assault at West Point Ken Kelsch. Photo Credit: Dennis A. Livesey.

Assault at West Point Ken Kelsch and his crew. Photo Credit: Dennis A. Livesey.

Assault at West Point Ken Kelsch behind the lens in June 1993.

Ken Kelsch at the Chateau Marmont in 1993.

Ken Kelsch and crew behind the camera on Dangerous Games.
Photo Credit: Dennis A. Livesey.

Madonna, Jack Mac, Ken Kelsch, and Don Cerone. Photo Credit: Dennis A. Livesey.

Ken Kelsch and team on Dangerous Games. Photo Credit: Dennis A. Livesey.

Ken Kelsch and Dennis A. Livesey. Photo Credit: Dennis A. Livesey.

Dennis A. Livesey and Abel Ferrara Behind the lens on Dangerous Game. Photo Credit: Dennis A. Livesey.

Andrea Dorman, Rob Kummert, Jennifer Loader, Dennis A. Livesey, Ken Kelsch, and Steve Treadway. Photo Credit: Dennis A. Livesey.

Andrea Dorman, Steve Treadway, Ken Kelsch, and Rob Kummert. Photo Credit: Dennis A. Livesey.

Big Night Camera crew. Photo Credit: Dennis A. Livesey.

Ken Kelsch setting up shot for Big Night. Photo Credit: Dennis A. Livesey.

Ken Kelsch and Big Night crew. Photo Credit: Dennis A. Livesey.

Ken Kelsch and Andrea Dorman. Photo Credit: Dennis A. Livesey.

Big Night 1995 Minne Driver and Ken Kelsch birthday cake.

Behind The Imposters Ken Kelsch and Dennis A. Livesey. Photo Credit: Dennis A. Livesey.

 The Greatest Gangster Movie You've Never Seen

Ken Kelsch and Jennifer Leitzes in 1997. Photo Credit: Dennis A. Livesey.

Ken Kelsch in 1999. Photo Credit: Dennis A. Livesey.

Now and Again: Ken Kelsch and Faith Price. Photo Credit: Dennis A. Livesey.

Now and Again: Martgaret Colon and Ken Kelsch. Photo Credit: Dennis A. Livesey.

Ken Kelsch and his camera crew in New York with the World Trade Centre behind them. Photo Credit: Dennis A. Livesey.

It Had to Be You: JJ Jacobs, Dennis A. Livesey, Ken Kelsch, Steve Treadway, and Kory Solomon. Photo Credit: Dennis A. Livesey.

Happy End: Audrey Tauto, Ken Kelsch, and Dennis Livesey. Photo Credit: Dennis A. Livesey.

Ken Kelsch and crew on Return to Sleepaway Camp. Photo Credit: Rob Koch.

Dennis A. Livesey and Ken Kelsch at Vietnam Memorial Washington DC. Photo Credit: Dennis A. Livesey.

Ken Kelsch and Dennis A. Livesey at screening for The Addiction. Photo Credit: Dennis A. Livesey.

Dennis A. Livesey, Ken Kelsch, and Kyra Sedgewick.

Dennis A. Livesey and Ken Kelsch. Photo Credit: Rob Koch.

Dennis A. Livesey with Ken Kelsch Last Time. Photo Credit: Dennis A. Livesey.

Chapter 3

Framing the Legacy: A Tribute to My Father, Ken Kelsch, Through the Lens By Chris Kelsch

Chris Kelsch checking the frame. Photo Credit: Ken Kelsch.

"I want to be a director of photography"

Although I did not really understand what it was, when asked what I wanted to be when I grew up, I would always respond that I wanted to be a DP. I think ultimately I wanted to be a badass creative like my father, Ken Kelsch.

Ken's story was such a unique odyssey that there will likely never be someone quite like him. He "oozed" (one of his favorite words) a combination of extra macho masculinity mixed with an intelligent and sensitive wisdom. Ken's background in the military as MACV SOG, studies in the seminary as a child, and other extraordinary life events compounded with Abel Ferrara's own one-of-a-kind likeness have created an entire library of standout work.

Being a professor in addition to a DP, Ken taught a lot of different subjects relating to film but would often joke his favorite subject to teach was himself. If you gave him a platform, showed him respect, and opened up your ears to him, he would give you the keys to his creative force. On the flipside, if he found you unworthy, he would tell you thoroughly, using some of the most colorfully harsh vocabulary and crush your ego.

Danny Stewart came into my dad's life at a time when Ken was deeply reflecting on his terrestrial and cosmic existences. He was recently diagnosed with terminal cancer, was coping with the losses of my mother, his sister, and the end of a long and dramatic relationship. His health was preventing him from participating in the long chaotic shoots and culture that his life was built on. The scary diagnosis he was given finally had the grim reaper, that he had denied so many times, knocking at his door. Through his curiosity, knowledge in film, and respect that he showed to my father, Danny received the keys from Ken at one of the most vulnerable points of his life.

Through the trust and friendship Stewart built with my father and his own film expertise, Danny has the most unfiltered and honest perspective of Ken's approach to work. His passion and ambition to share Ken and Abel's work fills me with gratitude for Stewart, as that badass and creative work my father achieved is given a respectful platform to live on. Those who have earned and sustained a relationship with Ken Kelsch are rewarded with a treasure of knowledge, and we are privileged to get an understanding of Ken's work with the insider perspective he trusted to Danny.

I will certainly never be as badass or creative as Ken, but his uniqueness is what made him special and we will never lose his resonance when we have those like Danny Stewart celebrating and analyzing his craft.

Chris and Ken Kelsch. Photo Courtesy of Chris Kelsch.

Chris and Ken Kelsch thumbs up on a boat. Photo Courtesy of Chris Kelsch.

Ken and Chris Kelsch at a game. Photo Courtesy of Chris Kelsch.

Chris and Ken Kelsch enjoying some food at the game. Photo Courtesy of Chris Kelsch.

Ken Kelsch Brewing a fire. Photo Courtesy of Chris Kelsch.

Ken Kelsch ready for some corn. Photo Courtesy of Chris Kelsch.

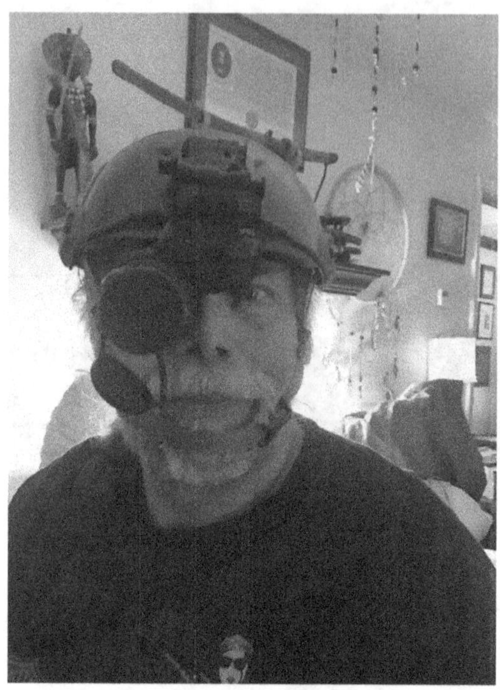

Ken Kelsch military gear. Photo Courtesy of Chris Kelsch.

Ken Kelsch with a sundae. Photo Courtesy of Chris Kelsch.

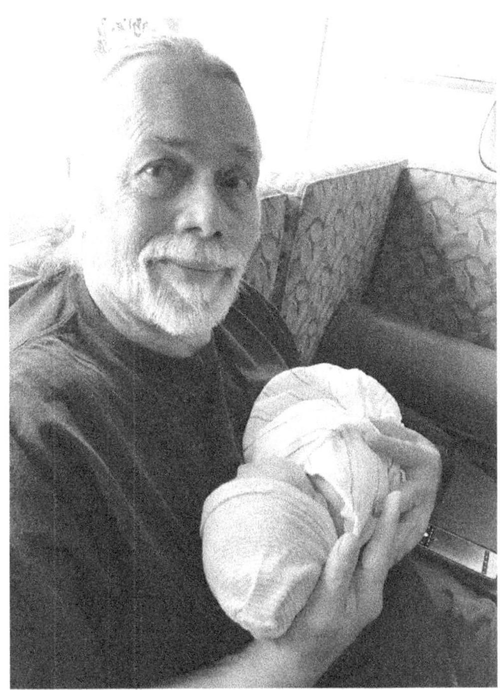

Ken Kelsch with grandchild. Photo Courtesy of Chris Kelsch.

Ken Kelsch with grandchild. Photo Courtesy of Chris Kelsch.

Chapter 4

A Cinematic Collaboration: Christopher Walken and Abel Ferrara

Publicity photo of Christopher Walken in stage play, Hurlyburly.[v]

"I always think that in movies or on stage, two people can be talking to each other–the audience doesn't necessarily have to know what they're talking about, just so long as they know that YOU know what you're talking about."– Christopher Walken[4]

The partnership between director Abel Ferrara and actor Christopher Walken has resulted in some of the most memorable

____

4   *https://www.imdb.com/name/nm0000686/quotes/ Christopher Walken IMDB Quotes*

films in American independent cinema. Both artists are known for their intense, uncompromising approaches to their craft, and their collaborations explore themes of violence, power, guilt, and moral ambiguity. Ferrara, often working on the fringes of Hollywood, brings a raw, gritty sensibility to his films, while Walken's distinct screen presence adds layers of complexity and menace to his characters. Together, they've created a body of work that stands out for its emotional depth, philosophical weight, and striking visuals.

Their collaborations include King of New York (1990), The Addiction (1995), The Funeral (1996), and New Rose Hotel (1998). These films, while diverse in genre, all share a common concern with exploring the darker aspects of human nature and society.

The first of Ferrara and Walken's collaborations, King of New York, redefined the gangster genre with its brutal honesty and complex characterization. Walken stars as Frank White, a recently released drug lord who returns to New York City to regain control of his empire. White, however, is not a typical crime boss; he's a paradoxical figure who uses his ill-gotten wealth to fund hospitals and help the poor, blurring the lines between villainy and heroism.

Walken's portrayal of Frank White is magnetic and unsettling. With his cold stare, unpredictable demeanor, and calm ruthlessness, Walken brings a sense of moral ambiguity to the character. White is both feared and respected, a man who navigates the city's underworld with the same ease as he engages in philosophical musings about justice and power. Ferrara's depiction of New York as a chaotic, morally gray landscape perfectly complements Walken's performance, turning King of New York into a modern crime epic that examines the corrupting nature of power and the blurred boundaries between good and evil.

Ferrara's direction in King of New York showcases his ability to merge genre filmmaking with deeper thematic concerns. The film isn't just about crime; it's about the allure of power, the decay of institutions, and the personal cost of ambition. Walken's Frank White becomes a symbol of this decay, a man who represents both the potential for social good and the inevitable corruption that comes with unchecked power.

In The Addiction, Ferrara and Walken ventured into the horror genre, but with a philosophical twist. The film is a black-and-white meditation on sin, guilt, and the human condition, using vampirism as a metaphor for addiction and moral corruption. Lili Taylor stars as Kathleen, a philosophy graduate student who becomes a vampire after being bitten, and soon embarks on a bloodthirsty spree that echoes the compulsions of an addict.

Walken plays Peina, a reformed vampire who has learned to control his addiction by abstaining from human blood. His character serves as a mentor figure to Kathleen, offering a philosophical perspective on the nature of sin, evil, and redemption. Walken's performance is hauntingly restrained; Peina is a figure who embodies both wisdom and menace, a being who has transcended his vampiric instincts but remains deeply aware of the darkness within him.

Ferrara uses The Addiction to explore themes of guilt and moral responsibility, central concerns in much of his work. The film, with its stark visuals and philosophical dialogue, offers a unique take on the vampire genre, using horror as a vehicle for existential inquiry. Walken's Peina, with his philosophy, adds a layer of intellectual depth to the film, making The Addiction a thought-provoking examination of human weakness and the possibility of redemption.

In The Funeral, Ferrara and Walken returned to the crime genre but with a more somber, introspective tone. The film is set in 1930s New York and revolves around the Tempio family, a group of Italian-American mobsters who are mourning the murder of their youngest brother, Johnny. Walken plays Ray Tempio, the eldest brother, who is grappling with his grief while also plotting revenge against those responsible for Johnny's death.

Walken's portrayal of Ray is deeply emotional and nuanced. Unlike the cold, calculating Frank White of King of New York, Ray is a man overwhelmed by guilt and sorrow. He is haunted by his role in the family's violent criminal lifestyle and is torn between his desire for revenge and his growing realization of the futility of violence. Walken masterfully conveys Ray's internal conflict, balancing his character's exterior with moments of intense vulnerability.

Ferrara uses The Funeral to examine the emotional toll of crime and violence on the human soul. The film, with its mournful tone and philosophical underpinnings, is less concerned with the mechanics of the mob world and more focused on the psychological and spiritual consequences of living a life steeped in violence. Walken's performance is key to this exploration, as his character becomes a tragic figure caught between loyalty to his family and the moral weight of his actions.

New Rose Hotel, the final major collaboration between Ferrara and Walken, is an adaptation of a William Gibson short story and delves into the world of corporate espionage and seduction. Walken plays Fox, a manipulative and cunning fixer who enlists Willem Dafoe's character, X, to carry out a plan to seduce and betray a corporate scientist. The film is a minimalist, dreamlike exploration of trust, loyalty, and betrayal, set against a backdrop of futuristic intrigue.

Walken's portrayal of Fox is one of his most enigmatic performances. Fox is a charming but untrustworthy figure, a man who operates in the shadows and uses others to achieve his ends. Walken imbues the character with a sense of ambiguity, making it difficult to discern Fox's true motives or loyalties. His performance, like the film itself, is elusive and atmospheric, contributing to the overall sense of unease and ambiguity that permeates New Rose Hotel.

Ferrara's direction in New Rose Hotel is more experimental than in their previous collaborations, relying on mood and tone rather than plot to convey its themes. The film is a slow, meditative exploration of betrayal and desire, and Walken's performance anchors it with a sense of cool detachment and danger. While New Rose Hotel received mixed reviews upon release, it has since gained a cult following, with many viewers appreciating its abstract style and philosophical undertones.

The cinematic collaboration between Abel Ferrara and Christopher Walken has produced a body of work that is both dark and complex, reflecting their shared interest in exploring the moral ambiguities of life. Ferrara's films often deal with the psychological and spiritual consequences of violence, addiction, and power, and Walken's performances bring these themes to life in deeply unsettling and compelling ways.

Walken's ability to embody characters who are both charismatic and deeply flawed makes him the perfect actor to inhabit Ferrara's morally complex worlds. Whether playing a drug lord, a vampire, or a grieving mob boss, Walken brings a sense of depth and unpredictability to his roles, elevating Ferrara's films beyond mere genre exercises into profound explorations of the human condition.

Their collaborations have left a lasting mark on independent cinema, offering audiences a series of films that are both emotionally resonant and intellectually challenging. Together, Ferrara and Walken have created a cinematic legacy defined by its uncompromising vision and its fearless exploration of the darker sides of human nature.

Chapter 5

Interviews

Interview with Director - Abel Ferrara

Danny Stewart: So, looking back on your collaboration with Nicholas St. John, what inspired you to delve into the themes of crime and family dynamics in The Funeral?

Abel Ferrara: Nicky St. John wrote The Funeral. I got the script from Nicky. We grew up together. I've known him since I was 14 years old. It's like, life experiences, and a million conversations, and doing shared movies, and me and Nicky played music together. There was just so much that we shared in life. But Nicky wrote that himself. So, when The Funeral came to me, it was a complete script. I didn't work with him on the script. The script was done. Our families originated in Campania, which is a county of the state of Napoli. But he was from the farms outside of Napoli. Two different places, but we had the same culture.

Danny Stewart: Interesting. Was he Italian-American as well?

Abel Ferrara: Yeah. Nicky spoke Italian, he lived in Italy. He was the first one to go there. He married an Italian woman. But this was basically stories he had heard. He comes from Mount Vernon, his family. Mount Vernon was on the edge of New York, the outer ring of New York City. So, the two inner-city Italian neighborhoods were Morris Avenue and Arthur Avenue in the Bronx, and Mulberry Street in the West Village and Manhattan. Mount Vernon was like a small town. So, this was basically the story of the mafia, Italian-Americans doing gangster shit in a small town. During the 30s, but in a small town. Because most of these stories are either set on Mulberry Street, or they're all in New York City. Rarely do they tell stories. Because

Italians were all over the country. I mean, there was a big mob in New Orleans, Providence, Milwaukee, all these places.

Danny Stewart: There was the Irish mob as well. It was a whole culture.

Abel Ferrara: Yeah. So, a lot of this was based on true stories, or stories he heard.

Danny Stewart: I think it was based on his uncles; I believe.

Abel Ferrara: Maybe not so much based. I'm sure he's heard these stories, and I'm sure these stories are told. How much is truth, how much is not, who knows? But it's a work of fiction. It's a screenplay. Nicky wrote scripts, he didn't write books. At the time.

Danny Stewart: Do you keep in touch with Nicky?

Abel Ferrara: Nicky and I have not. He stopped working in the business not long after this. This was one of his last ones.

Danny Stewart: I think it's really fascinating, the whole story itself, the whole dysfunctional family, the whole political landscape as well. The Vincent Gallo character, that whole movement, and communism. It was so fascinating. It was a different take on the gangster genre.

Abel Ferrara: Nicky is brilliant. He's brilliant, and the script is brilliant. It's as simple as that. But he was also with me. When we made the films, he was there all the time.

Danny Stewart: I mean, it was a great script. And you live in Rome, so I'm guessing there's still very much corruption, and the mafia still very much exist as well.

Abel Ferrara: Yeah, whatever you call it. The violence on this Earth is off the hook.

Danny Stewart: The Funeral had such a powerhouse cast. What an ensemble you had. I love the philosophizing of the gangsters. The great speeches in The Funeral with Chris Walken's

character. And I remember the line in the film is, "Once you pull the trigger, there's no going back." And it's so true. Especially in that life.

Abel Ferrara: Yeah. And it's a metaphorical line too. You know, once you create. You perform the action, that has its consequences.

Danny Stewart: Absolutely. And Victor Argo had a small role, but he was in The Funeral as well. He's since passed away. What were your memories of Victor?

Abel Ferrara: Victor came from the Scorsese world of the films that meant so much to us. My memory of Victor is playing guitar with him. For a Puerto Rican guy, he was a big country western fan. We'd sit and play George Jones songs. That's the relationship I had with him. He was a great friend of Harvey. He was in all our movies in the way he was in all of Marty's movies.

Danny Stewart: That's right. He was in Taxi Driver. I remember he was in Smoke with Keitel as well. He'd always make appearances. That's wonderful. And also, the female cast, you had Gretchen Mol, Annabella Sciorra, and Isabella Rossellini, great actresses. What were your memories of working with them? They played the women in the lives of these gangsters, and I think they did terrific work.

Abel Ferrara: You don't see a lot of that side of it in these kinds of movies, you know? That's what the movie is about. Nicky writes the screenplays. And this is classic filmmaking. This shit isn't done on the set. He's writing the scripts, and he pushes us to find. The better the script, the better the character, the more you're reaching out to find the people who can do it. Annabella, we knew. She was a friend, and so swas Gretchen. Gretchen's brother was actually an assistant editor with us. Isabella, we adored. Her we didn't know. We reached out outside of our world a little bit for Isabella, Benicio, and Vinny. I didn't know Vinny or Benicio before we cast them. It was a classic. We took on the aura of a 40s movie, or a 30s movie. Even the way we shot it, the lens choices, the camera choices, and the static camera.

Danny Stewart: When I was talking to director of photography Ken Kelsch, he was telling me it was very much against his normal documentary style. That's why I really like it. The lighting and the production design by Charlie Lagola, the costume design. It was immaculate.

Abel Ferrara: This is part of the 90s. We weren't just shooting like The Addiction. Bad Lieutenant was kinda low-budget too. So, in this situation, it was the height of the independent New York film movement, so we had the money to pull off this. If you're doing a 30s movie, you obviously gotta have some money.

Danny Stewart: What were your memories of Chris Penn? Obviously, he had a lot of demons going on at the time, and he did fantastic work in the film.

Abel Ferrara: Watching the guy. You know, when you see that performance. What can you say? He's on fire. But the fire went out. And it's tough to watch. He lived to 40.

Danny Stewart: He was young. And it was quite a tragedy.

Abel Ferrara: It was a tragedy. Chris was special in so many ways. In just so many ways.

Danny Stewart: I think this is his best performance. Very intense. I remember, the ending was powerful. Did he lose his mind? Could he cope with life without his brother? Had he gone mad? All these things come in. And I think it was a haunting ending. It was very powerful.

Abel Ferrara: Well, one person in the family is always the crazy brother, and that's who he was. And with him playing that, and knowing his history and knowing who he is - but he's an actor, he's an actor playing a role. And again, he's one of the reasons you're writing this book, because these people came together, Nicky and all the people you're talking about, we came together at the perfect time. I mean, we were together, but the money came together, the script was written, there were people appreciating that script, and they gave us the money to pull it off. It was all a perfect storm. And none of us allowed it to be let down. I mean, a lot of crazy things happened. I was as out there as Chris Penn was. But the rest of the team were. Kept the fucking, you know. Kept the car on the road. We brought the shit back to shore. And that's the movie.

Danny Stewart: Absolutely. Looking back now, how do you feel about it in your whole resume of your whole filmmaking? Where would you put it? Would you put it up high?

Abel Ferrara: I don't look at my movies like that. I think of it as a document of a time in a life, I guess. But how did you come upon this film?

Danny Stewart: So, I had done film studies, and I bought a DVD, and it had a double disc of The Addiction and The Funeral. So, I had watched both with my dad. I had written a whole thesis on Bad Lieutenant. I watched it with my father, and I was just absolutely blown away. I thought the whole period, the look, the style, the performances, it was just… It's funny, because when I was speaking to Kenny, he said that out of all the Abel films he worked on, this one was the most accessible, in terms of… If you could call it accessible. But I just think it was… That's why when I was talking to Ken, I was saying, he loved the title that I got for the book, "The Greatest Gangster Movie You've Never Seen," because it really is.

Abel Ferrara: Why do you think people have never seen it?

Danny Stewart: I don't think it got distribution, or didn't get promoted enough. There's all these things. It didn't get a good release. I think it deserves a re-release. It deserves a special edition. It deserves a revival.

Abel Ferrara: It's out there. It's out there somewhere.

Danny Stewart: And I suppose every film you do is different. And Abel's films aren't the same. You do different films. You don't just stick to a niche, or go for the commercial, "Let's make a big Hollywood film," you know. They're more personal films. And they're deeper. They're working on other levels. And much more artistic. And I suppose you're someone who's like Pasolini, in a way. Obviously you were influenced by him.

Abel Ferrara: Yeah. I'm influenced by him; he's not influenced by me.

Danny Stewart: Exactly. And you've had that effect on other people, like myself, and… I remember in my film studies class, my teacher was like, "Very good choice." I had written a thesis on Bad Lieutenant. I've written loads of stuff on the film, and just analyzed it. And that's what I'm gonna do in the book as well, analyze The Funeral. I just think that this film, out of all your films - everyone always talks about King of New York, everyone talks about Bad Lieutenant, everyone talks about The Addiction. And they're all great, but I think The Funeral deserves more of a say in your filmography. Do you ever miss America? I'm sure you don't.

Abel Ferrara: If I miss America, I get on a plane and go there. I have options. I don't miss it that much. If I was missing it, I'd be living there. I'm not in exile, I'm living in Europe because it's my choice. It's where I wanna make films; it's where I can do the kind of films that I want, where directors are respected for what they are.

Danny Stewart: Totally. It's much more on the artistic side of things, and I think people appreciate the work a lot more. I completely agree. Obviously, I'm from the UK as well. I love European films. Even though the whole industry has changed.

Abel Ferrara: Yeah, everything is different. The whole world. Since COVID, everything started changing, total flux. What's here today is gone tomorrow.

Interview with Director of Photography Ken Kelsch

Danny Stewart: Please discuss your collaboration with Abel Ferrara and how it initially began.

Ken Kelsch: My collaboration with Abel initially started with the film Driller Killer and they were shooting on the weekends. In the beginning, I wasn't involved, so they had another cinematographer who was friends with Abel. However, they decided they wanted to shoot straight through instead of just on weekends. Abel contacted NYU and asked for their best cinematographer and luckily, I was nearby as I had just graduated from NYU and Abel was living on 18th Street. I was sitting in the office of NYU at 7th and 2nd. I walked on over.

Abel called me on a Saturday, and I went to meet him. We discussed the project and shared some not-so-great Mexican pot. He offered me $100 a day to work on the film. At the time, I had my own lights, a van, and my two Doberman dogs. Abel's loft was on the ninth floor of an industrial building and the eighth floor was occupied by a metal caster named Osborne, a great guy. Since the elevator was out of order, I ended up leaving my dogs in the car and keeping the gear there too.

We shot for 20 days, and towards the end, we filmed at Max's Kansas City, which was nearby. We managed to gain access to the venue by telling everyone there would be a free open bar, although there wasn't one. We filmed the audience first before they realized there was no free booze and left, and then we moved onto the stage. The place was a mess with cockroaches and shit, but we didn't have much choice. We shot for 50 hours straight, barely catching any sleep. It was a blur of continuous shooting, and I don't remember much. We wrapped up the film without needing any additional shots, and that experience marked the beginning of our collaboration.

I volunteered my time and equipment to teach at a CETA course. Every Tuesday, when I wasn't working, I would teach these kids. My wife would take over when I had to work. I feel a bit guilty about it because the chances of them finding a job were quite low.

However, one of the guys, Felix Rivera, actually became a well-known gaffer in Los Angeles.

One day, Dale drove over to pick me up, and we went to the loft after watching Apocalypse Now. Watching the movie really upset me because, firstly, I was already dealing with PTSD at that time in my life. Secondly, the movie is supposed to be based on a guy who was in my old unit in Vietnam, the character portrayed by Martin Sheen. The character of Colonel Kurtz was based on a distorted version of Robert Rheault, the commanding officer of the fifth Special Forces Group, who had "gone native." It's interesting because, in a way, we had all gone native. We, SF guys, lived with the tribesmen, the Montagnards. I even got inducted into a tribe, wearing a loincloth and bracelets. These guys saved my life multiple times because they had been doing it for so long. I was just a young guy in my 20s doing these cross-border operations into Laos, Cambodia, and other non-permissive environments. It was usually just six of us against unknown enemies on the Ho Chi Minh trail.

The year 1968/69 was a full-scale war, with guys dying left and right. Some teams went in and were never heard from again. God knows what the fuck happened to many of these guys.

I carried a five frame 38 on the lanyard around my neck, because I knew that I wasn't gonna be captured, I would rather eat that fucking gun; if you gonna die anyways you may as well kill yourself before you're being tortured for days or years. I certainly knew quite a few and served in the company of the heroes. It was disturbing for me, and Tony Rowe was a great commander, was probably one of the best commanders of Pittsburgh. We were not technically in the fifth Special Forces Group. We were the special operations on rotation. So, the CIA ran us, and we were administratively underneath those guys. Colonel Warren, my CO, was phenomenal. Great guy ex-Korean Ranger. Terrific. Commanding officer had nothing but contempt for the SF guys because we weren't getting the support that we got. And this was after Tony Rowe left and at that time the

CO was not a favorite of Jack Warren. So, at any rate, I saw the movie, I said, this is insulting. This is like a drunken display of assholes and one thing I would say about my experience with SF, Special Forces guys are certainly different than most of what you would ever expect. These guys are not the Marines in the army. These guys are smart, intelligent. These guys were, they were possibly the smartest guys I've ever met in my life, maybe with a homicidal bend. But they were extremely smart, extremely facile, extremely brave, and dedicated guys. Although crazier than a shithouse rat. So, the whole idea of Martin Sheen, drunkenly stabbing himself on a piece of mirror was almost insulting to me, but it is what it is. I realized later on I've seen the movie multiple times. Look, my experience of Vietnam was totally different from anybody else's. You know? This is Ken's little journey over there and, certainly, it's funny because one day I ask Harvey Keitel, "What was it like being fired for Apocalypse Now?" He looked at me. His look said it all; it was like: What the fuck does Coppola know about Vietnam? It's true, you know, but he made an aesthetic decision. It's like the war and gangster films where they are unfolding of a certain dramatic staple. It's often visited, not done so well, all the time. But in this case, look, I backed away from it. I looked at it as sort of a war story written on acid. And it worked for me. Robert Duvall is great. They're sort of cartoon caricatures. Again, you'll never get what it's like to be in a situation like that unless you're in a situation like that. The movie is always going to come up short. So, at any rate, I was disturbed. I go over Abel's house smoking cheap Mexican crap. You know, $10 an ounce shit, not like they have today. Stems and seeds in, rolled up in the paper, and drinking cheap wine. We got to dinner. We get drunker. We're sitting down, Dale, myself and Abel. And he goes, "I want you to shoot the next one, Ms. 45." And then I said to him, "Well, how much?" He said, "Well, I'll give you a percent. Every week you're on I'll give you a percentage." Let's put it this way. Our finances were of scary sources. And what the fuck am I gonna do? Am I gonna go to Secaucus and end up with a pair of concrete shoes in the East River. So, I go, fuck, no, I want $1,000 a week. So, Abel stands up and has a look that says, why don't I just buy you a fucking Mercedes.

And for me, to not send him a free taekwondo lesson. I hit the table, broke the table and walked out. So, I didn't hear from him for eight years. After that I was doing a lot, I was doing commercials, and I was making a pretty good buck, as a Commercial DP, but you know, look, I didn't go to graduate school to sell soap. So, I wanted to get back into narrative films. And, you know, we ended up reconnecting. The first thing we shot together was the FBI Untold Stories, which he got fired from. And then we ended up doing Bad Lieutenant and we started working together again, so 14 films later here we are.

Danny Stewart: Initially, it was fascinating because the original intention was for Chris Walken to play the lead in Bad Lieutenant. However, he eventually had a change of heart.

Ken Kelsch: That movie the original script was 30 pages long. The movie is so bleak. I mean, it's really an exercise in despondency. One of the best things about it is that it shows you the isolation of the addict alcoholic, you can't live with the drugs, and you can't live without them. And how addiction will strip your soul. Harvey's amazing in it. To be honest, I never thought anybody could pull it off as well as he did. Siskel & Ebert wrote letters to Academy members they knew to vote for Harvey, but dealing with the whole NC-17 format, we didn't realize how difficult it is because you can't advertise in the movie section. You can't do this. You can't do that. There's a whole bunch of provisos, rules; they had this puritanical aversion of it. The first movie that was at NC-17 was Henry and June. And that was a stinker. I'm a Fred Ward fan and Henry Miller fan. That movie was a mess. And just didn't do it. And I think that Fred Ward was incredibly miscast, but this was much more interesting going through the Marvel Universe and seeing what Wolfman is doing today.

Danny Stewart: You also collaborated on Dangerous Game.

Ken Kelsch: I didn't do Body Snatchers. Abel called me up on Christmas Day. Ruined my fucking Christmas and said you're not going to do it. So, look Bojan Bazelli is a talented photographer. And he had a lot of money. And they were afraid to trust it to a guy who just shot a $2 million film, that whole thing was a mercy fuck on my part. I mean, my salary was pathetic. I basically gave away my lighting and grip. My guys were working for dirt. The teamsters were a drunken mess. Sometimes after shooting 12 hours I had to load my own trucks. Because they were too drunk to put my lights on the fucking truck. I would drive home and go to work the next day. It was an interesting exercise. I tell my students my job doesn't exist anymore. You're not going to make a living doing what I did. It's just impossible. The 90s were really the halcyon days of independent film in New York. *The Village Voice* was very kind to me a lot of times and basically called me the image of independent filmmaking in Manhattan, which was very complimentary. But the fact is, there weren't too many DPS, and that were gonna load their own truck after working a 12-hour day for dirt money on Bad Lieutenant. But I felt it was a great privilege in a way to participate in Keitel's phenomenal acting. It was truly a tour-de-force, and I don't believe anyone will ever replicate it. You would never find another actor who could have done the job the way he did it.

Danny Stewart: After Dangerous Game you had done The Addiction with Abel.

Ken Kelsch: The Addiction is my favorite film because I shot it black and white. Walken is always one of my favorites. He's a great pleasure to work with; Lily's a phenomenal actress. I love her. Edie Falco was terrific in it. Mike Imperioli has a small bit, another unrecognized underrated actor. The Addiction, which I did more of as a sympathy fuck and less money than Bad Lieutenant. I turned down a month-long trip to Asia to shoot something and I ended up getting a bounced check from Abel. But like I said, it's still my favorite film, shooting a black and white as a DP is incredible. It's an incredible experience. I don't recommend it. When I was doing The Imposters, Tucci was thinking of shooting black and white, like the Marx Brothers. And I discouraged it. And the reason I discouraged that is because I think that it really limits your audience. You want people to go out there and see it, what I do like about it, stylistically, I always like to consider myself a minimalist, for the most part, and source driven, but when you're going into black and white, you're immediately going to stylize the format because you're doing nine Shades of Grey, that's it. You're already separated. For me as a DP, I want to suck you into the frame, I want you to be sitting with your peripheral field, and I want you to be in my world, and I, as the director of photography, my photography is going to give you your world, you're looking through my eyes of what my version of reality is. So, if I'm source driven, I'm hopefully bringing you into a universe, which you accept, as fact. When you are in black and white, you're already deviating, it's different, you're in a different world. So, for you to make the leap into accepting it's a bigger step. However, aesthetically, you really have to light, and I was very happy when the manager of Duarte said to me, Ken you must have shot a lot of black and white, because, you know, you did a great job, my numbers were perfect, in terms of my black and white pack for the day. When I was doing the traditional photo chemical chain, and I had shot so much, so many black and white stills as an undergraduate and I had my first darkroom when I was 12 years old, I knew a thing or two about black and white photography, but there's a total difference between the fluid art and a single frame graphic representation of still photography. It's sometimes a cross purposes to one another because I want to bring you into Chris Penn's world in The Funeral, I want to bring you into the tragedy of Annabella Sciorra smoking a cigarette and trying to get out of the violence of this family. I want you to totally accept that. In black and white I'm making a statement, and I enjoy making a statement. It's not the same and in Bad Lieutenant, basically I wanted it to be like a documentary, but The Addiction no. The Addiction was, really, another of Lily's tour-de force and Walken with the great sequences as Peina he's terrific. This is the best thing about working with Abel. Despite that, sometimes we're ready to kill each other. His choice of actors Walken and Harvey are terrific. I also thought that in Dangerous Game Madonna, as much as she disliked the film because it wasn't four hours of her doing her thing, Abel got the best performance from her.

Danny Stewart: The collaboration just went from then onwards. Between all you guys, you know?

Ken Kelsch: It's an interesting, philosophical journey. Once again, screenwriter Nicholas St. John's philosophical exploration into mega-noma and Nicky's particular weirdness. A voice well-missed in the Abel Ferrara universe. So, all I can say is I wish Nicky was back. I haven't seen Nicky in years, and I hope he's doing okay.

Danny Stewart: Screenwriter Nicholas St. John, his apex was The Funeral.

Ken Kelsch: I thought so too. Dealing with his family and history. It was based on the three uncles he grew up with; you can tell that he's got a lot of personal affection for these characters. Nicky's a complicated guy. It interests me in movies and Abel too is moral imperative, moral dilemma, and this is moral dilemma. Our politics are pretty polarized, Abel and myself, but he's a guy who follows pretty much Hollywood mainstream.

Danny Stewart: It's funny you say that, because in the film The Funeral the politics are very polarizing, because you've got the three brothers. It's crazy.

Ken Kelsch: Right. The whole thing was crazy. The Walken character, I think, is much more of a straight-line gangster, as opposed to the left-wing Vincent Gallo character, who was trying to be on a social economic cutting edge. And maybe finding some sort of moral justification for his actions. All rebels are gangsters aren't they. This is part of part and parcel of the whole thing. I don't particularly ascribe to not buying into what's being dictated by the clergy or politicians. The minute they start living their own credos, their own agenda, something that is not apparently only for us and not for them, then maybe I'll pay fucking attention. And that's part and parcel of it. Mary Kane, the producer of all these films, would say we're rebels, and I don't necessarily agree with that I feel like I'm a rebel. There's a lot of me that's a traditionalist. I served my country for five years. I want my kids to succeed in their lifestyle. I want security. I want government to do the most important thing it should be doing, which is making us secure; it doesn't, everything's for sale nowadays. I don't want Big Pharma to be telling me what I should or should not be taking. I grew up in the 50s; I know what it's all about. I know that this isn't the America I grew up in. And I think that we have sacrificed a lot of stuff. My sister used to say that I was the libertarian who acted like a Democrat. And maybe that's true, I'm for freedom. Freedom of expression. I only did TV when I got divorced. I had to go with a fucking pay check. And I hated it. I gotta tell you, I hated every fucking second of it, selling myself out. Putting up with the crap that everybody's a boss thing in TV is so restrictive. It's not HBO. It's not watching The Sopranos; it's so restricting it saps the creativity out of you. In TV, coverage is king. The fact is that you got eight to ten days shooting your network TV series. Which could be interesting. The best thing about doing a long-term thing like Sopranos is that you can watch the characters more so than two hours. I mean, look at the continuing saga of the Marvel Universe, you have an opportunity to give your characters interesting tilts, but it doesn't happen. Because you're not dealing with reality. You're dealing with superpowers. When you're getting in trouble, your superpower solves it instead of reality. The reality of day-to-day existence in Peekskill in the 30s. In gangster land. That's kind of interesting. How do you do it? In the middle of the Depression, how do you survive? This is a question we're going to all have to ask ourselves in the future, unfortunately.

Danny Stewart: How long did you take to shoot The Funeral?

Ken Kelsch: Trying to figure out, so disjointed it was only like yesterday, to start finishing Big Night. Prepping for a week, shutting down for whatever time it was when I took my bike out to Sturgis and that pissed my wife off to throwing some T-shirts in the back of my Harley. Driving in North Dakota. Leaving her with the kids No wonder she divorced my fucking ass. Coming back and then going into work, brutal hours doing it. I think it's the most accessible of Abel's films. So, I was glad to be working. It's really an interesting take on gangsters. We shot around 25 days.

Danny Stewart: Where did you shoot the film?

Ken Kelsch: We shot in Brooklyn. Charles Lagola, I'm a big fan of Charlie, as a production designer. And I'll tell you why Charlie puts the money on the screen. He did a great job on The Addiction and on The Funeral. When we started out, we lost money, because we shut down, we lost a million dollars, because of our false start. We made a period piece for a $6 million budget. This is pretty fucking amazing. It was well done, and Charlie did a great job plus, the making of a period piece, just finding the cars doing this and doing that. And finding the props. It was very authentic. The authenticity was there. Being the guy who's lensing giving you, you're looking at this film with my eyes and Charlie's eyes, too. We're giving you in a modern neighbourhood, we're giving you a very limited select, period piece, we're showing you the city in a very constricted time frame. And it was not easy.

Danny Stewart: The ending of The Funeral was unexpected. Did Chris Penn's character lose his mind? Or did he get some sort of illness? Or was he mentally ill?

Ken Kelsch: Extremely, it was unexpected. So, you weren't prepared for it. It was very disturbing. Well, I think that you're just crushed by the guilt of it all. I've been going through the guys in my unit now. The ones that lived are dying right and left. I was at a funeral last

Saturday. I was at a funeral the week before that. People are dying, right and left. The despondency, that when your loved one passes away it's so brutal. My friend, Steve Kahn, had just passed; he gave me my first steady gig, working for this awful dance TV show when I was first starting out. It gave me a steady pay check that allowed me to pursue other ventures, and he is a guy I've known for 50 years. We called each other every day. He died of leukaemia. He's not there anymore. I wake up in the morning, sometimes I want to give Steve a call but Steve's dead. And it's like, okay, what do I do now? I mean, it's just a moment. My sister passed. And it was terrible, my ex-wife, who I'd reconcile with passed a year later. I was luckily available to take her to her treatment, which made up for time. I wasn't the best husband in the world, I was too busy making Abel Ferrara movies. When she got sick with the same thing that my sister had, blastoma, and she passed, I was there. I was there when she died. I was there when my sister died. These are privileges. It's a gift that you get as miserable as it is to watch someone slip away. I relate to looking at the coffin and incredible emptiness of that abyss you feel when someone who has had such an incredible part of your life. It's all of a sudden ripped from you. First thing, it's a kick in your brain and cortex. To remind you that there's a beginning and there's an ending. The first thing it does is say to you: buddy, you got a whole lot less in front of you than you got behind you. So, get your shit accomplished now, do the stuff that's important to you now. I talk to Abel almost every day; we're like dysfunctional brothers. I can't figure out where I would be without Abel in my life. It's a frustrating thing to say because, as he says to me, that his last two movies, well I didn't light it. To me, the heart and soul of cinematography is lighting. The Funeral it's not my normal Bad Lieutenant quasi-documentary look at stuff. It's a very stylized look. People ask me about my style of photography, I always say that I bring a different approach.

Where would I be without Abel? We've had the longest collaboration, when we're talking about the cinematography. Abel's biggest thing is he doesn't want to be artificial. I relate to that. You want truth in direction, you want truth in acting. I want truth in lighting. Unless I make the leap in The Addiction where I'm gonna be totally stylized, unless I make the leap in The Funeral where I'm making my lighting as a statement. I fucking hate the fact that you can go to your modern digital cameras and crank the ISO up to 3000. As a traditionalist in some respects, I like the fact that I'm lighting, once again, you are watching the movie through my eyes, and my brain is telling me what should be lit and what should be dark. I'm a guy who believes that dark is as important as the light. I want to control that. As a DP, my own issue is control. As a director, that may be your issue, control. Or sometimes as Abel likes to say, *"My decision is to let the actor make the decision."* Fine, great, terrific. I'm not a guy who believes in sound lighting. I don't believe in going to location and letting the existing lighting positions dictate how the film is gonna look. I want to have my heavy hand direct the crew to light it the way I see. And I did that in The Funeral. My buddy, Bill Pope, I went to grad school with was up for Bound and Roger Deakins, who won the Spirit Award for Fargo. To be in the company of those guys . . . I didn't win but to be mentioned in the same paragraph of those two, I was very proud.

Danny Stewart: What were your inspirations for The Funeral? Did you have any specific gangster films in mind that you wanted to light in a similar manner?

Ken Kelsch: My two favorite films are The Godfather and The Godfather Part II. Gordon Willis is undoubtedly one of my idols. The Godfather is an iconic film with magnificent cinematography, making it one of my top five favorites. Whenever I feel down, I can always rely on The Godfather parts 1 and 2 to lift my spirits. The sheer brilliance of Gordon's photography is truly awe-inspiring to watch.

Danny Stewart: Speaking of the gangster genre, there is one film in particular that stands out with its stunning lighting. The Road

to Perdition is exquisitely lit and shot, adding to its overall beauty.

Ken Kelsch: I recently watched this film, and it was truly stunning. The execution of it was flawless and breathtaking. The cinematography was particularly beautiful, thanks to the incredible talent of Conrad Hall, a two-time Academy Award winner. I've been a fan of his work, especially In Cold Blood, for a long time. The way he captures scenes in black and white is simply masterful. The guy is a true genius in his craft.

Danny Stewart: The movie Road to Perdition has a distinct artistic aesthetic, similar to that of The Funeral. Both films share a stylized visual approach in their photography. Also, Road to Perdition is set in the 1930s, just like The Funeral, further enhancing the shared atmosphere and sense of time.

Ken Kelsch: It does, its very well executed.

Interview with Production Designer - Charlie M. Lagola

Danny Stewart: How actively were you involved in scouting and selecting shooting locations for the film? Did you collaborate with Abel Ferrara as you had in previous projects? How did this film compare in terms of personal challenges and satisfaction?

Charlie Lagola: Actively, yes. How it kind of happened was Abel had called me first off when he had the script in hand and the potential to fund it. So we actually started talking and scouting locations together before there was even production funding available. There was also a location manager named Mike Nicodem with us at the time. Abel, Mike and I nailed down many choices by driving around together and pinning places we knew we could shoot for 1937 without creating a budget disaster. At the time VFX were very expensive and not a solution we could factor in, so we had to be careful about the location choices and also careful on how Abel could cover the scenes photographically without seeing something anachronistic. Abel was nervous about it as he had not ever made a period film and he said to me "you find it" and "don't let the movie look brown!" We had many discussions about that and the palette of the movie from that moment on. Producer Mary Kane had come on to the show, albeit late in prep, and was sceptical about how we could do 1937 on all these locations, for a reasonable price. We had it planned out and Abel said, "We're gonna shoot where Charlie says we're gonna shoot when Charlie is ready for us to shoot it." That was a very gratifying moment I must say. The faith and trust that Abel had with me was great. To your question about challenges and satisfaction, that moment was one of the most satisfying of my career. As we got into shooting, Abel would often be thrilled at what we had prepared for the actors and him to work with. Once he said, "Geez! I hope the direction can live up to this art direction." The family house (Walken's) by the way was the largest challenge of the show. The location was a great find, especially since it had a full lot side yard. We stripped out the actual kitchen, made our 1937 version, and then removed the exterior back wall of the house as a "wild wall" so cameras had space to shoot it. The side doors where Chris Walken makes his entrance into the living room from the side yard was actually a window we pulled out and built in a set of double doors. Color also was discussed between Abel, Ken and myself to a fine detail. Interior rooms were painted in super dark colors so to allow the actors' faces to be almost like a reverse silhouette yet with detail, so that the room or walls never were a value greater than that of the tone of the actors. This was also coordinated in detail with wardrobe. Any pop of color, a flower, a plate, a piece of jewelry was carefully selected and placed with intention. Kudos, by the way to Diane Lederman who was our set decorator on this project.

(Note: There is a folder of still shots in my portfolio online at www.charlielagola.com)

Danny Stewart: In terms of preparing for the film, did you rely on the screenplay, engage in discussions with Abel Ferrara, or conduct independent research? How did Ferrara's input shape the overall tone and appearance of the movie?

Charlie Lagola: We did tons of research. At that time we were able to physically go to the NY Public Library picture collection and find exteriors, interiors, people, and more in photos that existed from the 1930's. My team did a lot of seeking and looking for these as well as there was a store in NY that sold actual magazines and newspapers from the time period. We purchased these as part of our research and they were often in good enough condition to actually use on set as props and set dressing. We would board out photos of locations, vehicles, wardrobe, props, furniture, and more and pin these all up on the walls around the art department so all could see the items and tones and direction of what we were bringing to set. Early on, Nick Cage was intended to be in the movie, but that never materialized. However, in a meeting we had with him, as he wanted to see what we were up to, he and I were looking at photos of period cars we could get. There were examples of vehicles from 1920s through 1937. What we noticed was a definitive shift in design style of cars from box-shaped to a more streamlined fast back look that happened in the 1934-35 model years. Nick suggested we only use the more recent "fast back" look as a style choice and keep the "boxy" look out of the show. I thought it was a great idea as a style statement and onward we went so you'll see the cars that our main characters use are all post 1934. Abel's input at this stage of development often manifested in conversations about what not to do. From previous paragraph notes such as "don't let it look brown" or "no red"... "unless it' s in the flowers at the coffin" All background should be dark. Let's move more scenes to night from day. Abel generally leaves details up to the team yet there will sometimes be some specific things that upon immediate presentation feel wrong to him and he lets you know it. I found that this process with him informed our style a lot of what "to do," by being clear and decisive on what "not to do."

Danny Stewart: What are your recollections of working with such a talented ensemble cast?

Charlie Lagola: I loved that cast. My memory of them and what they put into it daily was inspiring in the sense that they were fully committed, fully committed to Nicky's script, fully committed to Abel's vision. A lot of that in my opinion came like a waterfall from the enthusiastic commitment by Chris Walken. He is a leader. I believe, surmise, the cast committed to bringing all they could bring because of Chris's commitment. They had to be aware and feel that commitment from him that then lifted them into better performances. Just my opinion from a behind the camera pov. That also permeated what they felt as their environment also. For example, a couple days before we had this big food set up at Ray's house, Annabella Sciorra (Ray's wife) talked to me and insisted she make some of the food herself and bring it to set. It was after all her house too as the matriarch of the family. Annabella made the broccoli rabe, and something else I can't remember. My wife, in real life, Italian, and also the script supervisor, made a cassata cake. There was this camaraderie between cast and crew at times where a symbiosis of effort, without hierarchy or ego, added to the basic desire to make a great movie.

Danny Stewart: With a plethora of gangster movies and period source material available, what specifically drew your attention and served as your inspiration? In what ways did you aim to push the boundaries of the genre and offer something unique?

Charlie Lagola: Abel and I in very early one-on-one conversations were wholly agreed we did not want to copy or even emulate what other gangster period movies were or had looked like. We came to the idea that we didn't have to fight with what we found if what we found was basically not wrong. I think he and I both felt that if we didn't "try too hard" we would end up with something feeling naturalistic and organic even if we were creating period.

Danny Stewart: How did you personally react to the final product of the film?

Charlie Lagola: Then and now it is still one my proudest accomplishments. The film looks as good as any Godfather movie, as any gangster movie, it's marvellously stylistic and many kudos and thanks to Ken Kelsch for the photographic style that gives it life. I can still look at that film today and every set/location and still know that we did it right. We did it well. We did it very well as a result of Abel's clear vision and a team that coordinated beautifully: Ken the DP. Mindy Eshelman, costume designer, and all our department heads and team.

Interview with Costume Designer - Mindy Eshelman

Danny Stewart: When did you start working with Abel Ferrara?

Mindy Eshelman: I started with Abel on Bad Lieutenant, Body Snatchers, and Dangerous Game. I was the assistant costume designer on those three films. Then I designed The Addiction, The Funeral, and The Blackout. I began prep on New Rose Hotel, but funding was not secured so I had to leave for, I think, Office Space.

Danny Stewart: What was your first impression of Abel Ferrara when you first met him?

Mindy Eshelman: [Laughs] I met Abel at the Chateau Marmont during the initial prep for Bad Lieutenant. I was fresh out of graduate school and new to LA so my first impressions were more just observation. I was very quiet, and he was loud, but open. He had a tremendous energy and was excited about the work. There was a passion he exuded that brought us all onboard. I had no idea what I was getting into, but I was game.

Danny Stewart: Which costume took the longest time to design and create?

Mindy Eshelman: No costume in particular was the difficult, but The Funeral was the most costume heavy show of Abel's because it took place in the early 30s and also the late teens. The need to be flexible and living in the knowledge that the script was more of an idea than a plan. The joke was that "scripts tend to confuse people"… either Walken or Abel said that. There was always someone showing up that Abel wanted to put in the film, and since it was period, it was a challenge to keep the integrity of the period. There was lots of research involved. Abel was concerned that while it was a period film, once you were into the story the feeling of period should take a back seat. It was important that it didn't end up looking like Merchant Ivory. M-L are beautiful films where the clothes sing. The Funeral was not to be that. The look needed to be raw and real.

Research was Weegee and personal photo albums from the time and area, so real people in real clothes.

We had just done The Addiction which was shot in black-and-white. Abel loved the look, but it was hard to get distribution for a black and white film. So, The Funeral was to be black and white but shot in color. I held the pallet a very tight palette.

Danny Stewart: Can you discuss your memories of the cast and each character's specific costume wardrobe for The Funeral?

Mindy Eshelman: The cast was wonderful to work with. Each had their own process. With Isabella, she was so lovely and gracious. Chris Walken specifically asked for me to find the most beat-up, worn-in pair of Brogans because it was really important to him that his feet be as comfortable as possible. It made sense for his character but usually we would buy new and then distress them to appear worn. He wanted shoes that someone else had really worn in. So, we did, and we would carry these on-camera shoes to set whenever he was called to camera. And he would wear his Nike drawstring mocs. Any shots where you don't see his feet, he is wearing his Nikes. I wanted to add that Edie Falco, pre Sopranos, showed up to her fitting on roller blades. I adore her and it was great to work with her again after The Addiction. Do you also have that Nicholas Cage was to originally supposed to play Ray. Chris came in towards the end and was wonderful to work with him again. I ran over to The Public Theater where he was in rehearsal to start conversations about Ray.

Danny Stewart: Do you prefer actors openly expressing their opinions about their costumes, or do you prefer them to be indifferent?

Mindy Eshelman: I always want actors to develop the character with me. I see it as a three-way triangle between the actor, director and myself. We all have our focus and together the goal is bringing the actor to the story and the character and find where they intersect. Through lots of conversation with each other we are more successful in doing our work. In solid collaborations, the director's focus is the overall vision for the story, the actor focuses on their puzzle piece of their character, and I gather the looks of all the characters and puzzle them into the story. It is amazingly satisfying when it all works.

Danny Stewart: What was your reaction to the film?

Mindy Eshelman: It is a beautiful and powerful film. The improvised and nuanced performances and Abel's willingness to continue to edit and rearrange the story always has me surprised once it is cut. There are always so many layers in Abel's films that one pass is never enough. The script is only an idea and what ends up in the film is devised from the collaboration of many artists. Ken, Charlie, and I created a world that held up to all the continued devising of the piece. I was happy that it made people think and that you are shining light on it. It is dark and violent, but there is so much more than that.

My only negative reaction, to be honest, was being disappointed when I saw the original poster. It does not look like our movie. Chris is not wearing anything remotely similar to our film. Their looks were very modern and polished, far from the gritty world we created. Not sure why they went that way, but when they did re-releases, they used images from the film.

Interview with Producer – Mary Kane

Danny Stewart: Did you get a chance to re-watch The Funeral?

Mary Kane: Yes, I did. I got the DVD and I watched it. You know, it was quite a long time ago, but I watched it. We can go through your questions. I hope I'm not a disappointment in this.

Danny Stewart: I don't know how long it has been since you've spoken to Abel.

Mary Kane: We've spoken. For many years, we didn't speak, but in the last couple of years, I saw him - he was in for the retrospective he had last year at the American Cinematheque that he had in LA. I saw him then, and we've spoken a few times since. And there was something else that came up recently, and I said, "You should talk to this person." I forget what it was. And he said, "No, no, you talk to him." It wasn't you. Watching The Funeral, the cinematography is brilliant. After not seeing it for so many years, and now I've watched it a couple of times, bits here and there, that kind of stuff, the cinematography is beautiful.

Danny Stewart: So, you're originally from New York as well, aren't you?

Mary Kane: Yes. I grew up in Rockland County, which is outside the city on the Jersey side. On the other side of the Hudson.

Danny Stewart: Ever since COVID, it's just got worse. Things have accelerated. I'm sure you know, the whole film industry has changed completely. It'll never, ever be the same again.

Mary Kane: The last 10-12 years were a bit of a fluke, I think. I come from the time when there were a few television stations and a few films, and the streaming, it was just - I mean, I didn't stop in 10 years. And believe me, the years before that, I definitely had times when I wasn't working. But the streaming, everyone was working. And now very few people are working.

Danny Stewart: The films that you were involved with, they'll never be made that way again. They'll never make Bad Lieutenant again. You couldn't make it now, you know?

Mary Kane: No.

Danny Stewart: You wouldn't get away with what you did.

Mary Kane: No.

Danny Stewart: You'd be arrested.

Mary Kane: Right. They'd be coming after us.

Danny Stewart: When did you get involved in the film industry? What motivated you?

Mary Kane: So, here's the back-story. I grew up in Rockland County, and my first year of college was at Rockland - have you heard this story about Abel?

Danny Stewart: Go ahead.

Mary Kane: So, my first year of college was at Rockland Community College. You know the colleges in the States. And this was in the days you just went and signed up. It was a community college. You just went and signed up. So, he grew up in Peekskill, which was on the other side of the Hudson, but he also went to Rockland Community College the first year. We're the same age. We graduated high school at the same time. The second year, Rockland Community College had this program - and I didn't meet him the first year. It was a big school, no one lived there. He lived in a place over by the school because he was further away. I lived closer.

Danny Stewart: So, that was with Nicky St. John?

Mary Kane: Yeah, Nicky St. John. But Nicky grew up in Peekskill. They went to high school together. So, the second year, Rockland Community College had this program to send the kids abroad. And again, you just went and signed up. You didn't have to give your right finger. It wasn't a big deal. You just had to pay more than you were paying for the college. So, I signed up, and Abel signed up. We were at this school outside of Oxford called Alvescot. It was run by expatriates, and the guy who ran the place - it was a tiny little school. The guy who ran the place was this aristocrat. And the idea was to get the kids from this community college to see something of the world. So, I met Abel there. He was making films then. Then, when we came back - he only stayed a semester, I stayed a year, but I came back. I made enough working three weeks at a supermarket than I had worked at through high school and my first year of college, to go back for another semester. And I worked in a bookshop… Anyways, he went back to Rockland Community College. So, this was our third year of college. They started a new school, SUNY Purchase, which has now become, over the years, a big theatrical school. They've got a dance company; they've got a theater company. But it's part of the state system, it's not a private school. So, it was the first year. So, we both ended up there. But I knew him. And then, we were living in a - you know, it was back in the day, when people - not communes per se, but we were living together. Not as a couple. We were never a couple. There were six or seven of us in the house. So, I think I took another semester. I forget. We finished Purchase, but he was making movies then. So then, I just started working with him. I had other jobs, he was raising money. I left, I went and lived in the Caribbean for a couple of years, but came back, I think - some of these things I get mixed up, but I came back to do Ms. 45, went back to the Caribbean, came back. And at some point, I think it was the late 80s, I moved to LA.

Danny Stewart: So, you started out doing Ms. 45. I see that you were credited as an associate producer, so you were there in the early days, you knew Abel.

Mary Kane: Yeah.

Danny Stewart: And what about Zoe Lund? What were your memories of Zoe on Ms. 45 and Bad Lieutenant?

Mary Kane: My memory of her was…First of all, you have to understand, Abel did most of the casting. And he's brilliant at casting. When you look at The Funeral, come on. We made this for two cents, look at the actors? The actors are unbelievable. And Ms. 45, he found her, and she was 17. I remember sitting around the table with her parents, who had to sign the contract. She wasn't old enough to sign this contract. And she just had the look. And Abel thought…I forget if I read this - we were all in a loft building on 18th Street and 5th Avenue. I can tell you real estate stories you don't wanna hear.

Danny Stewart: I can imagine.

Mary Kane: I'll tell you the story he told at the retrospect. I was going out of town with my daughter, so I only went to one of the movies at the retrospect, and it was Ms. 45. So, we were all living in this loft, and he looked through the peephole and saw her coming off the elevator, it was one of these elevators that had a gate. It was a very funky building. It's not funky anymore. And he just looked at her, and he saw her face. And he said she was it. He found her. Abel found her.

Danny Stewart: She was unbelievably talented. She was obviously very beautiful. And it's very sad that she passed away very young.

Mary Kane: Very young.

Danny Stewart: But obviously, like Abel, they were very artistic and creative. Crazy, but highly creative.

Mary Kane: And fighting demons. You know what I mean? I think that's one of the reasons Abel and Kenny became so tight in later years, because Kenny was very instrumental in helping guys get sober. This was before the kids were born.

Danny Stewart: That's right. I remember Kenny telling me, "Where would I be without Abel?" They were like dysfunctional brothers. And obviously, those guys together, they made and shot unbelievable films. And you were part of that legacy as well.

Christopher Walken, he's an unbelievable talent. An absolute legend.

Mary Kane: It was after his Vietnam Movie, wasn't it? I'm pretty sure of the fact that we found him after Deer Hunter. I mean, everyone remembers that scene.

Danny Stewart: Totally. It was The Deer Hunter, and I remember that he had another great performance in a film called At Close Range with Chris Penn. He was the father of Sean Penn and Chris Penn. I mean, he was unbelievable. He was so evil in the film. It was an unbelievable performance. And so, after King of New York, that's when you produced Bad Lieutenant. In my eyes, that's a masterpiece. It's an absolute masterpiece. Harvey Keitel, just unbelievable. I don't think anyone could replicate that performance. Absolutely masterful. I mean, he should have got an Oscar. He should have won an Academy Award. It was just unbelievable.

Mary Kane: But the type of film…It wasn't mainstream.

Danny Stewart: No, no, this wasn't mainstream at all. This was underground, arthouse, indie. These were just… It's a shame. We'll never get films like this again. I'm glad you produced these films. So, Bad Lieutenant, what were your memories like working on that? I mean, it must have been quite an experience.

Mary Kane: Yeah. I don't remember much, I gotta tell you. I don't remember much. Nicky wrote the stuff, which was brilliant. It wasn't a committee, or in television where you have these rooms. There was none of that. So, the stuff was brilliant. And I always felt my job — and that's because he taught me this, because I didn't have any other experience, really — was to try to give him what he wanted. And we had to pay bills. Back in the day, I would do equipment deals on a handshake.

Danny Stewart: For the film, for the processing and stuff like that?

Mary Kane: You can see it - I mean, I can always tell the difference. You can see it when you watch Bad Lieutenant. That's film. But Kenny was brilliant, because…Today, on digital, what the cameraman is getting, you're seeing. There's not this mystery of… And Kenny would say, whatever the ASA, and the aperture, all this stuff.

Danny Stewart: It was like a documentary. It was like you're watching real life. It was reality. It wasn't like…The way these films now are digital, the film was raw. You could smell it.

Mary Kane: And I don't remember…Now, all the television stuff I do, you never have less than three cameras. I don't think we ever even had two cameras. And when you see the way the stuff is shot, The Funeral, come on, it's beautiful. These actresses are unbelievable.

Danny Stewart: On The Funeral, what were your memories of the cast? The ensemble was unbelievable.

Mary Kane: I mean, on these low-budget things there were no divas. You know what I mean? The diva thing didn't work. So, I don't remember any issues. I remember on… Maybe it was the thing with Lawrence Fishburne. We didn't have trailers; we didn't have all this stuff. I remember one time, we were putting the actors in what was like a bikers' joint. And I remember saying to Laurence - Larry, he was Larry then. I said, "You okay?" And he was like, "Yeah, yeah, I'm okay." It's like craft service nowadays. There would be a little table with donuts that you could bounce and coffee. And this would be on the streets of New York. Because if you had a camper, you had to have a driver… I don't remember picking up after… It was very different than how the business has changed, and how I worked on bigger things. The television stuff I've been doing for the last 10 years, there's 250 people a day. And that wasn't the off-set people. That tells you the scope of things. So, I don't remember any… As I said, my memory is that they were all great, they were happy to be there, there were no divas. I remember being in Dangerous Game, and we were meeting Madonna in the loft.

And again, this is a funky loft. The whole building was industrial. It's not anymore. And she came with her own water. That was smart.

Danny Stewart: I can imagine it wouldn't be the place that she would be caught dead in.

Mary Kane: I'll tell you a story Abel told about the loft at the screening of Ms. 45. I forgot about this. So, they were doing a documentary about him in Italy. So, they went back to the loft. I don't know how he got in, but he got in. So, when we were there… This the 80s, right? And he said there was mutiny in the home building when the rent went from $500 to $600 a floor. Meanwhile, this was 2000 square feet. This wasn't a tiny little place. But there were potters, and it was supposed to be industrial, but this is just when people were starting to live there. Now, the place is done to the nines. 5th Avenue and 18th Street in Manhattan, 2000 square feet. So, we were paying $500, $600. And sometimes there were a lot of us living there when we were in the middle of a movie, and he said the guy now is paying $19,000 a month.

Danny Stewart: What? That's crazy.

Mary Kane: Exactly. And there was one toilet. I remember my bed - I had doors that we had picked up on the street. Someone was selling away doors. That was how I made a bedroom. This kind of stuff. $19,000. I said, what does this guy do? He said he was a rich kid.

Danny Stewart: He must have been. How can anyone afford that? Unless you're a millionaire.

Mary Kane: Right, right. And I don't remember this, but he said that the whole building was mutinying when the rent went from $500 to $600. And there were potters in there who were living and working there, ceramicists, this kind of stuff. That was how…What SoHo in New York used to be; well, it's no longer. It's a 2000-square-foot palace.

Danny Stewart: Back to The Funeral, after watching the film again, what was it like viewing it again after all this time? I mean, the performances are amazing. Chris Penn had a lot of demons at the time, like a lot of the people Abel cast. But they're just unbelievable.

Mary Kane: He was unbelievable. And I love the thing you sent me about Kenny, how he was saying - I didn't get this at the time, how he related it to the fact of - from his Vietnam experience, not wanting to be the last guy left, or how you felt guilty of living when your fellow people die.

Danny Stewart: Exactly. Like haunted.

Mary: Yeah. Haunted. My memory is, they were great. I remember being in Little Italy, which was really Little Italy back in the day. I had to go in and make some deals for the street, one of the bars, and it was an illegal gambling place. I was so happy, because I was young, and I felt like this was an adventure. And the guys were great, but I had to go into this place and sit down and make a deal. Again, with a handshake. There wasn't a lot of paper. You weren't doing a contract for every little thing. That's the kind of stuff I remember.

Danny Stewart: Memories of Isabella Rossellini.

Mary Kane: Yes. Lovely. Lovely, lovely, lovely.

Danny Stewart: And Annabella Sciorra.

Mary Kane: Lovely. They were happy to be working.

Danny Stewart: Gretchen Mol as well.

Mary Kane: Gretchen Mol. Happy to be working. They knew what they were coming into. Abel wasn't shy. There wasn't pretense going on that this was gonna be something else.

Danny Stewart: No, they knew what they were in for. You had Benicio Del Toro. Edie Falco had a small role. She was in The Sopranos, but she had a minor role in The Funeral as well.

Mary Kane: My memory is that everyone showed up, we weren't waiting on the actors. I don't even remember where they did their hair and makeup. And these women look so beautiful, right?

Danny Stewart: They were stunning.

Mary: Just amazing.

Danny Stewart: I mean, I love that especially it's such an authentic gangster film as well. The screenplay was influenced by Nicky, who wrote the screenplay, it was based on, or it was inspired by his uncles. So, it was quite a realistic take on gangsters of that era, of that time. And the photography, the costumes… What's a shame is that these were indie films. These were small, low-budget films, so they never really get seen by the masses. And I've always thought The Funeral is one of the greatest gangster films, and no one's ever seen it. Well, it's not being seen by as many people as it should be. The ending is so haunting.

Mary Kane: So haunting, right. And you didn't see it coming.

Danny Stewart: It was so unexpected. You were like, what the hell? It was risky… It was Abel, so you know it's gonna be dark. And it really was.

Mary Kane: And Nicky - It was right off the page. Did Abel say, was Nicky on set much? I don't remember.

Danny Stewart: I think he was more involved on this than on any of the other ones. So, I think he was on set for some of the time. And I think this was a personal screenplay. It was the screenplay, it was unbelievable. It was on the page, right?

Mary Kane: Right. It was definitely on the page. It wasn't like anyone was improvising. I know every member on Abel's set, a lot of conversations about script. No, in recent years on sets, the actors will come…They just got down to it. And also, it was tick-tick-tick. You don't have that kind of time on these low-budget things. You gotta do it.

Danny Stewart: You guys went through it all, so it's a time of your life, and your career. How does it feel after all this time, looking back?

Mary Kane: That's a great question. Especially at my age, this is what I've been doing, looking back. You know, it feels good in some ways. My new mantra these days is "stay on the positive," and how life is serendipitous. Abel was always very supportive of me. I ended up with him. I was a big feminist in the 70s and at school, and he was supportive. "Talk to her, she'll tell you." He'd always push people in my direction. If it was in my purview. It wasn't like I was telling him about the script or the - you know what I'm saying? He was always very encouraging.

Danny Stewart: Do you ever see Nicky? Whatever happened to Nicky?

Mary Kane: Nicky left the business. I don't know if it was after The Funeral. Yes, I'm in touch. Nicky still lives in Peekskill. And I'm in touch with Nicky. We talk once in a while. He was a teacher for many, many years. He still lives in Peekskill. And when Kenny passed, I was the one that let Nicky know. Jackie Mack, I'm sure you've heard that name. He lives in Peekskill also. They've never moved from the hometown that they grew up in.

Danny Stewart: Ken Kelsch, just listening to him, you could write a film about his life. It was just like Abel. These people are characters.

Mary Kane: True characters.

Danny Stewart: The likes of which will never be again.

Interview with Actress Isabella Rossellini

Danny Stewart: I've been working on this book for a while now and I was very close with Ken Kelsch, the director of photography, who passed away. And he was one of my inspirations for the book. A truly amazing talent.

Isabella Rossellini: And the way he can hold that camera and move it and control it, yeah it was really rare.

Danny: My sister passed away also. I've dedicated it to Ken and my sister.

Isabella Rossellini: Oh, that is lovely. Oh, I'm so sorry for your losses, but this is so wonderful, too, that you're creating a book with them in mind and celebrating them.

Danny Stewart: So, prior to The Funeral, had you seen any of Abel's films?

Isabella Rossellini: So, all this was so long ago that I forgot. I'm pretty sure that I had seen some films, and I'm pretty sure that once I am offered a film, I generally, yes, I read the script, but I generally go and try to see films, all the films that I can from the author, because you can't judge from a script. You know, a script can vary. A good director can make a mediocre script very good, or a mediocre director can make a very good script into a very mediocre film, so I always read the script and watch their films. So, I did accept the film, because I liked Abel's work.

Danny Stewart: What specifically drew you to the role of Clara in the funeral?

Isabella Rossellini: I think what I liked best, I hadn't seen the film in a long time. It's not just films that I've seen a lot. So, I don't really like to see, to look back, because it makes me always melancholic. Colleagues have died, or it brings you, you know, there's always something sad. So, I never really watched my films. Abel, he's a fantastic artist, but he doesn't really have an enormous box-office appeal. So, his films are not really seen that much. I have seen Blue Velvet in my life maybe two or three times, because eventually there was the 30th anniversary, and they had a screening at MOMA, and they asked me to present it, so I sat there and looked at it. But generally, I don't look at my films.

But what I remember that I liked so much about the script, it was through the family life, through a family life of three brothers, there were three stages of integrating in America, it seemed to me. And there were these kinds of ways of becoming an American from being an Italian. And the mental anguish and the loss of identity and the reacquired values from another country. That's what I remember I liked so much. And my character, I think, was married to the middle brother, the one that was most tormented. We were the kind of hybrid that were born in Italy. I remember improvising a scene where there is the funeral, talking to the priest. I'm talking about how you find Pinoli in the streets of Italy. You don't have to buy them here in America. They're very expensive. All of that was improvised.

Danny Stewart: Interesting.

Isabella Rossellini: But I thought it was something plausible that people would say, when they are nostalgic of their country. And things were so much better there. And we left because, yes, there was this problem. So, when I had to improvise, I improvised in what I thought the people would say when they are caught in between being linked to a country that they come from but yet not integrated in a country that they now belong to.

Danny Stewart: Interesting. Because, as well, this was 1939. So, this was in the Depression era. And it was, I think it was very authentic, your costumes and the style. A different take on the genre. The family, it was dysfunctional.

Isabella Rossellini: Oh, my God, yeah. (Laughs) The least to be said. Very dysfunctional.

Danny Stewart: How would you describe your working relationship with Abel Ferrara?

Isabella Rossellini: Well, it was an incredibly chaotic set. But Ken Kelsch was very calm, and all the other people that worked with Abel said, oh, that's the way it is. Sometimes we didn't even know, I didn't know, when he said, action, and when he said, cut. Because everybody was talking, everybody was screaming. It was very chaotic. But then I look at Christopher Walken, and he seemed calm, and Ken was calm, and they kept saying, that's the way it works, that's the way it works. So, I stayed in character. I stayed in character as much as I can, because I don't know when the camera is rolling. But that's helpful for an actor. You don't have to come in and out, in and out of character. So also, I'm Italian. I grew up in Italy, so I'm very familiar with the demeanor, the culture. So, it wasn't a big stretch for me to play the character. I particularly liked the scene of the husband raping her. I think nowadays we recognize that rape can exist among married people. But at the time, I think it was considered, a husband can do whatever he wants. What do you mean? The husband is making love to you. He likes it this way. That's the way it is. So, I particularly liked that scene. I thought that scene was moving.

Danny Stewart: It was very effective, yeah. That's another thing I liked about it as well, is that the women in the film, it was a different take. Usually in the genre, the women are kind of sidelined. But I liked how it kind of delved into the women's lives just as much as it did with the men. And I think that, like you say, I think that was quite an effective scene. I liked how Annabella Sciorra would confront Christopher Walken's character saying, "You're gangsters and there's nothing glamorous about it."

Isabella Rossellini: Right, and I remember me commenting on, oh, you're having a lipstick, red lipstick, it's a funeral. This would have been something, I don't even know that Annabella knew it, she had a red lipstick. But it gave me the opportunity to improvise and being the older person that was, still attached to the tradition. In Italy, you would not go, maybe today, but then you would never, in 1939, you would never go to a funeral or in church with a red lipstick. So, those were the things that gave me the opportunity to improvise the little scene. But what I liked most about the film, it was the stages of integration in America, or even maybe in American violence, but that's the way I saw the film, that's the way I saw the film, really. The story of how to become an American.

Danny Stewart: Abel, who's Italian-American, and Nicky St. John was also Italian-American, the screenwriter.

Isabella Rossellini: The script was fantastic. It was one of the best scripts I've ever read.

Danny Stewart: It was very authentic, and what I liked about the film was that it was very intense, and it had a somber tone. I guess this is the atmosphere on set, it reflected the mood of the film.

Isabella Rossellini: The set was completely chaotic. Completely chaotic. Because the film was very good, and Abel's films were very good, but he shoots in a complete chaos that threw me.

Danny Stewart: You had a stellar cast. I mean, you had Christopher Walken, Annabella Sciorra, Vincent Gallo. What was it like working with all these actors?

Isabella Rossellini: It was great. At the time, Christopher Walken was the most known. And none of us had established our career. We were establishing our career, but none of us were as known as maybe today when we have our own resume of more films. So, we weren't as known. But they were kind of the New York cool artists, and I loved to work with them and be associated with them. I had great admiration for all their work.

Danny Stewart: Well, that's right. You had Benicio Del Toro, as well, I remember.

Isabella Rossellini: Yeah.

Danny Stewart: I don't think you could get that cast now. It would cost a fortune.

Isabella Rossellini: (Laughs) I can tell you that actors have a sense of who they work with, and they can select their script. Sometimes people think, oh, there's an agent that manoeuvres your career. Not at all. Abel is always, how you say, looked like the damn director. The crazy.

Danny Stewart: The crazy director.

Isabella Rossellini: And all of us were attracted. He's the crazy director, and all of us wanted to work with him because we were attracted to his talent. We saw beyond his chaotic set. We adapted to the chaotic set. To make this film, which I thought was a very good film. A very, very good film. And it deserved more success.

Danny Stewart: I think it's a masterpiece of the genre.

Isabella Rossellini: It's good, me too. In fact, it's one of the films that I'm most proud of.

Danny Stewart: I find that the ending of the film was haunting. Very shocking. With Chris Penn's character who has lost his mind.

Isabella Rossellini: It becomes an American tragedy. The madness and the violence.

Danny: As Christopher Walken's character says in the film, once you pull the trigger, there's no going back. And especially in that life, it's a cycle of violence. I just thought it was powerful. I remember that I was re-watching the film, I remember you were begging, your character was begging, Chris, please, no, don't, don't do this, don't do this. And then he shoots himself. And I just remember it was shocking. It wasn't like The Godfather, not that I don't like The Godfather, it's a good film, but The Funeral wasn't glamorized. And I think that's what was

so refreshing, Isabella, that it was, just a completely different take on gangsters, and that's why I liked it. It wasn't a Scorsese thing; it wasn't a Coppola thing.

Isabella Rossellini: It was family. A crazy family. That's what I loved about it.

Danny Stewart: It delved into these themes of family, loyalty, violence, mortality.

Isabella Rossellini: Well, I didn't grow up in America, but of course I'm taken back by the culture of violence that we do not experience in Europe. There are many similarities between Europeans and Americans in the way of living, but the guns and the violence is very far from Europe. That doesn't mean that we don't have any murders, but nobody has a gun. Nobody is wanting a gun, nobody thinks it's good to have a gun so that you can defend yourself, like in America. It's a sacred right to defend yourself if somebody steps on your lawn.

Danny Stewart: It's everywhere, isn't it?

Isabella Rossellini: It's really shocking. Oh my God, it's shocking to us Europeans and we can't really get our minds around it. Abel captured that stupor about the violence and that possibility because guns are available, that somebody at the funeral can pick up a gun. It wasn't polished, it wasn't sophisticated gangster, it was just a family and the family dynamics.

Danny Stewart: That's what I loved about it. It was the family, the brother, the dynamics were fascinating. The other thing that I liked, Isabella, as well is the younger brother, he was interested in politics.

Isabella Rossellini: Yeah, to me it was these three different paths to leaving your culture of origin and becoming American. That's what it was to me, the film was about, the path to become an American, but then it's also to become a crazy violence of America. I haven't seen the film in a long time, so I can only tell you right now what I remember liking about the script and liking when I saw the film, and it was this becoming American, of a family that came from another continent, Italy, which I know very well. So, it was easy for me to pray, to rosary, and improvise. They didn't have to have a consultant to say, how do you pray, how do you hold the rosary. There were so many things that I knew because I'm part of it, because I grew up in Italy.

Danny Stewart: And your family as well. That time in the 30s is when a lot of people migrated; there was a lot of migration.

Isabella Rossellini: I was born in the 50s, but of course the migration was very remembered. It was after the war that Italy became a rich country. Before the war, Italy was like today, Gaza, Syria, so we were migrating. A lot of Italians migrated to find fortune and eat, basically, because Italy was such a poor country. It became a rich country after the war, and I was born a few years after the war, but of course the memory of the misery and the memory of the war and the memory of the poverty that plagued Italy for a century, I was very familiar with.

Chapter 6

The Rossellini Family

Isabella Rossellini au festival de Cannes. Photo Credit: Georges Biard.[vi]

Isabella Rossellini's involvement in The Funeral carries a rich legacy, given her family's cinematic history. Daughter of famed Italian director Roberto Rossellini and Swedish actress Ingrid Bergman. Roberto Rossellini was one of the most prominent directors of the Italian neorealist cinema with films such as Rome, Open City (1945), *Paisan* (1946), and Germany, Year Zero (1948). Ingrid Bergman won three Academy Awards, two Primetime Emmy Awards, a Tony Award, four Golden Globe Awards, BAFTA Award, and a Volpi Cup. She is one of only four actresses to have received at least three acting Academy Awards. She made three films with

Alfred Hitchcock: Spellbound (1945), *Notorious* (1946), and Under Capricorn (1949). Rossellini and Bergman made five features together: Stromboli (1950), Europa '51 (1952) Journey to Italy (1954), Fear (1954), and Joan of Arc at the Stake (1954). In 1999, the American Film Institute recognised Bergman as the fourth greatest female screen legend of Classic Hollywood Cinema.[5]

Photo of Ingrid Bergman and Roberto Rossellini.[vii]

"In order to really create the character that one has in mind, it is necessary for the director to engage in a battle with his actor which usually ends with submitting to the actor's wish. Since I do not have the desire to waste my energy in a battle like this, I only use professional actors occasionally."

–Roberto Rossellini [6]

Critical Reception: Rome, Open City

"Rossellini's message of unity against injustice, wish for peace and hope for the future remains incredibly relevant

---

5   *"AFI's 100 Years ... 100 Stars". American Film Institute. https://web.archive. org/web/20061020084914/http://www.afi.com/tvevents/100years/stars.aspx*

6   *G., Anthony. "'Free' Cinema Italiano @ NGA:"Trip to Italy" by World Famous Director Rossellini." Meetup.*

and timely even today as the spectre of Fascist seems alive and well."- Clotilde Chinnici: Loud and Clear Reviews[7]

"One of the toughest, bleakest, war films ever made, this Roberto Rossellini classic simply couldn't be any other way."- Kevin Maher: Times (UK)[8]

"Rossellini forever changed the way we look at movies. By shooting just six months after World War II, he was able to film Italy's recovery through actual bombed out buildings, using a mix of professional and non-professional actors for authentic results."- Asher Luberto: L.A. Weekly[9]

"Handheld cameras tremble with the urgency of open wounds and violent emotion in Roberto Rossellini's 1945 drama of the Italian resistance to the capital's occupation by Nazi Germany."- Richard Brody: New Yorker[10]

Critical Reception: Paisan

"More ambitious in its structure than Rome, Open City."- Matt Brunson: Film Frenzy[11]

"Visually creative, emotionally involving look at the turbulent transition to liberated Italy in 1945."- Michael E. Grost: Classic Film and Television[12]

---

7   *Clotilde Chinnici Loud and Clear Reviews https://loudandclearreviews.com/rome-open-city-film-review/*

8   *Kevin Maher Times (UK) https://www.thetimes.com/culture/film/article/rome-open-city-1945-review-a-tough-powerful-wartime-drama-2hw0v9gkm*

9   *Asher Luberto L.A. Weekly https://www.laweekly.com/they-come-in-threes-the-best-trilogies-to-stream-right-now/*

10 *Richard Brody New Yorker (September 5, 2014) https://www.newyorker.com/goings-on-about-town/movies/rome-open-city*

11 *Matt Brunson Film Frenzy https://thefilmfrenzy.com/2017/07/19/view-from-the-couch-kong-skull-island-open-city-t-j-hooker-etc/*

12 *Michael E. Grost Classic Film and Television https://mikegrost.com/ross.htm#Paisan*

"Effectively maintains the rough-hewn, in-the-streets feel of neorealism, and in its best moments it feels like something captured, rather than something produced!"- James Kendrick: Q Network Film Desk[13]

"Has a passion, unlike a newsreel, that resonates and its authenticity as an important document of history cannot be denied."- Dennis Schwartz: Dennis Schwartz Movie Reviews[14]

Critical Reception: Germany Zero One

"Rossellini is perhaps the only filmmaker in the world who knows how to get us interested in an action while leaving it in its objective context. Our emotion is thus rid of all sentimentality, for it has been filtered by force through our intelligence."- André Bazin: Esprit[15]

"The colossal rubble of Berlin is not just an analogue to the collapse of the social order but an amazing sight, and the movie makes you feel the weight of every smashed facade and fallen stone."- David Denby: New Yorker[16]

"Short and very downbeat, this hits the irony buttons rather too much but is still an uncomfortable, powerful film."- Kim Newman: Empire Magazine[17]

"The documentary footage of a decimated Berlin is still enormously powerful, especially when compared to the

---

13 *James Kendrick Q Network Film Desk https://www.qnetwork.com/review/3898*

14 *Dennis Schwartz Dennis Schwartz Movie Reviews https://dennisschwartzreviews.com/paisan/*

15 *André Bazin Esprit - Bazin at Work: Major Essays and Reviews from the Forties and Fifties ISBN 10: 0415900182*

16 *David Denby New Yorker https://www.newyorker.com/magazine/2006/11/27/agony-of-defeat*

17 *Kim Newman Empire Magazine*

coverage of that other vanquished, but unscathed, capital in Rome, Open City."- David Parkinson: Radio Times[18]

Poster for 1941 film Dr. Jekyll and Mr. Hyde.[viii]

---

18 *David Parkinson Radio Times https://www.radiotimes.com/movie-guide/b-rp6dbi/germany-year-zero/*

**Lobby card featuring Spencer Tracy and Ingrid Bergman in
Dr. Jekyll and Mr. Hyde.**[ix]

Poster for the 1941 film Rage in Heaven.[x]

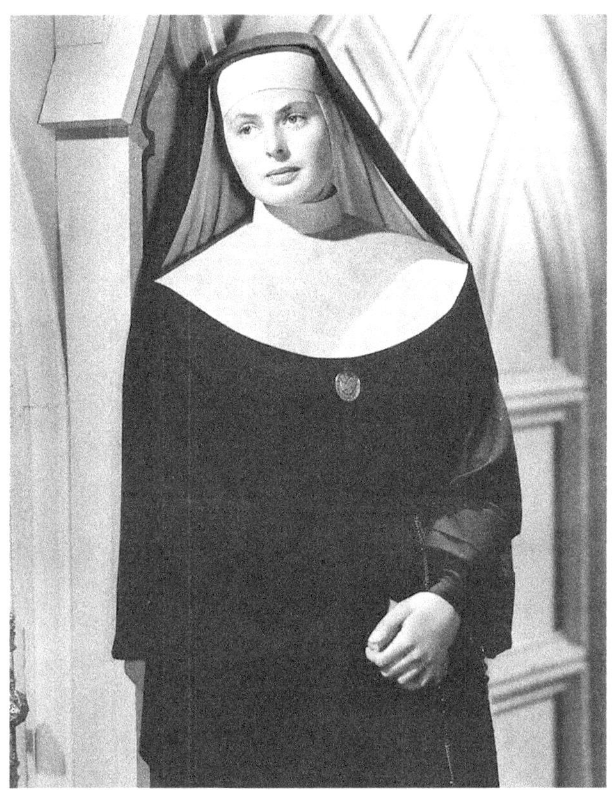

Ingrid Bergman in American drama film The Bells of St. Mary's (1945).[xi]

Screenshot of Ingrid Bergman in credits section of Casablanca trailer.[xii]

Original theatrical release poster for the film Casablanca (1942).[xiii]

Original press release publicity photo of Ingrid Bergman for film Gaslight (1944).[xiv]

Theatrical release poster for the 1944 film Gaslight.[xv]

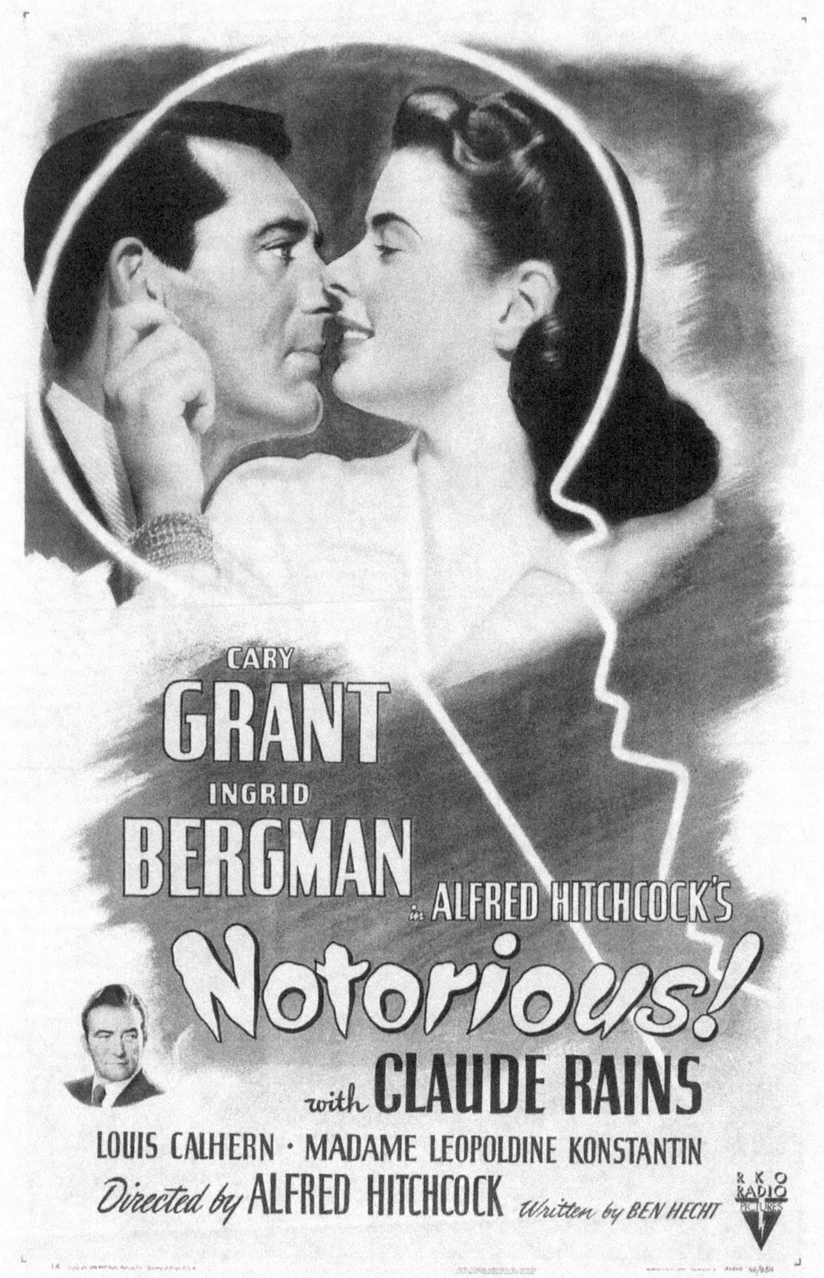

**Theatrical release poster for Alfred Hitchcock's 1946 film
Notorious.[xvi]**

Publicity photograph for the movie Notorious (1946), featuring stars Cary Grant and Ingrid Bergman.[xvii]

Cary Grant, Ingrid Bergman & Alfred Hitchcock on the set of the spy noir film Notorious (1946).[xviii]

Publicity Photo of Ingrid Bergman from the 1946 film Notorious.[xix]

Roberto Rossellini Filmography

- *La Vispa Teresa* (1939) - short
- *Il Tacchino prepotente* (1939) - short
- *Fantasia sottomarina* (1940) - short
- *Il Ruscello di Ripasottile* (1941) - short
- *The White Ship* (1941)
- *A Pilot Returns* (1942)
- *The Man with a Cross* (1943)
- *Rome, Open City* (1945)
- *Paisà* (1946)
- *L'Amore* (1948)
- *Germany, Year Zero* (1948)
- *Stromboli* (1950)
- *Francesco, giullare di Dio* (1950)

- "Envie, L'Envy" (segment of *Les Sept péchés capitaux*) (1952)
- *The Machine to Kill Bad People* (1952)
- *Europa '51* (1952)
- "Ingrid Bergman" (segment from *Siamo donne*) (1953)
- "Napoli 1943" (segment from *Amori di mezzo secolo*) (1954)
- *Dov'è la libertà...?* (1954) - abandoned, completed by studio
- Journey to Italy (1954)
- *La Paura* (1954)
- *Joan of Arc* at the Stake (1954)
- *India: Matri Bhumi* (1959)
- *Il generale Della Rovere* (1959)
- *Era Notte a Roma* (1960)
- *Viva l'Italia!* (1961)
- *Vanina Vanini* (1961)
- *Anima nera* (1962)
- "Illibatezza" (segment from *Ro.Go.Pa.G.*) (1963)
- *The Night of Counting the Years* (1969) - producer
- *Da Gerusalemme a Damasco* (1970)
- *Anno uno* (1974)
- *Il messia* (1975)
- *Beaubourg, centre d'art et de culture Georges Pompidou* (1977)

TV films

- *La Prise de pouvoir par Louis XIV* (1966)
- *Idea di un'isola* (1967)
- *Socrates* (*The Philosophers*, 1971)
- *Rice University* (1971)
- *Pascal* (*The Philosophers*, 1972)
- *Agostino d'Ippona* (*The Philosophers*, 1972)
- *Cartesius* (*The Philosophers*, 1974)
- *The World Population* (1974)
- *Concerto per Michelangelo* (1977)

- *L'India vista da Rossellini* (1959)
- *L'Età del ferro* (1964)
- *Atti degli apostoli* (1969)
- *La lotta dell'uomo per la sua sopravvivenza* (1970)
- *L'Età di Cosimo de' Medici* (1973)

Ingrid Bergman Filmography

- Munkbrogreven (1935)
- Swedenhielms (1935)
- Valborgsmässoafton (1935)
- Intermezzo (1936)
- Dollar (1938)
- A Woman's Face (1938)
- Only One Night (1939)
- The Count of the Old Town (1939)
- Intermezzo: A Love Story (1939)
- Rage in Heaven (1941)
- Adam Had Four Sons (1941)
- Dr. Jekyll and Mr. Hyde (1941)
- Casablanca (1942)
- For Whom the Bell Tolls (1943)
- Gaslight (1944)
- Saratoga Trunk (1945)
- Spellbound (1945)
- The Bells of St. Mary's (1945)
- Notorious (1946)
- Arch of Triumph (1948)
- Joan of Arc (1948)
- Under Capricorn (1949)
- Stromboli (1950)
- Europa '51 (1952)
- Fear (1954)
- Journey to Italy (1954)
- Joan of Arc at the Stake (1954)

- Elena and Her Men (1956)
- Anastasia (1956)
- Indiscreet (1958)
- The Inn of the Sixth Happiness (1958)
- Goodbye Again (1961)
- Hedda Gabler (TV) (1963)
- The Visit (1964)
- The Yellow Rolls-Royce (1964)
- Stimulantia (1967)
- Cactus Flower (1969)
- A Walk in the Spring Rain (1970)
- From the Mixed-Up Files of Mrs. Basil E. Frankweiler (1973)
- Murder on the Orient Express (1974)
- A Matter of Time (1976)
- Autumn Sonata (1978)
- A Woman Called Golda (TV) (1982)

Chapter 7

The Gangster & Crime Genre: A History

"The Italian gangster thing has become a form of the modern-day Western."– Armand Assante[19]

A gangster film is a specific genre of movie that centers on criminal gangs and organized crime. These movies showcase large criminal organizations or minor factions assembled for illicit endeavors. Unlike Western films, which typically portray lawlessness in the American frontier, gangster films primarily delve into urban criminal activities. Within this genre, audiences are captivated by the riveting narratives featuring these intriguing gangs and the heinous crimes they perpetrate. During the 1930s, three highly impactful gangster films emerged: Scarface, Little Caesar, and The Public Enemy. These movies are the finest representatives of their genre. The 1906 silent film *The Black Hand*, directed by Wallace McCutcheon, a pioneer cinematographer and director in the early American motion picture industry, who worked with the American Mutoscope & Biograph, Edison, and American Star Film companies, is considered by film historians to be one of the earliest surviving gangster films.[20,21]

One of the earliest full-length gangster films[22], *The Regeneration* (1915), is a silent biographical crime drama co-written and directed

---

19 *https://eu.southcoasttoday.com/story/entertainment/local/1996/08/03/armand-assante-proud-his-journeyman/50631974007/*

20 *Christine Bold, Joad Raymond, The Oxford History of Popular Print Culture: Volume Six: US Popular Print Culture 1860-1920, OUP Oxford, 2011, p.193*

21 *Daniel Bernardi, Michael Green, Race in American Film, ABC-CLIO, 2017, p.338*

22 *Nicole Hahn Rafter (2006). Shots in the Mirror: Crime Films and Society. Oxford University Press. p. 23. ISBN 0-195-17506-9.*

by Raoul Walsh. It was Walsh's first full-length feature film and stars Rockliffe Fellowes and Anna Q. Nilsson. The screenplay, adapted by Carl Harbaugh and Walsh, is based on Owen Frawley Kildare's 1903 memoir *My Mamie Rose* and the 1908 play adapted by Kildare and Walter C. Hackett.[23]

Poster for the 1915 film Regeneration, directed by Raoul Walsh.[xx]

23 *Aubrey Solomon (2011). The Fox Film Corporation, 1915-1935: A History and Filmography. McFarland. p. 229. ISBN 978-0-786-48610-6.*

    The Greatest Gangster Movie You've Never Seen

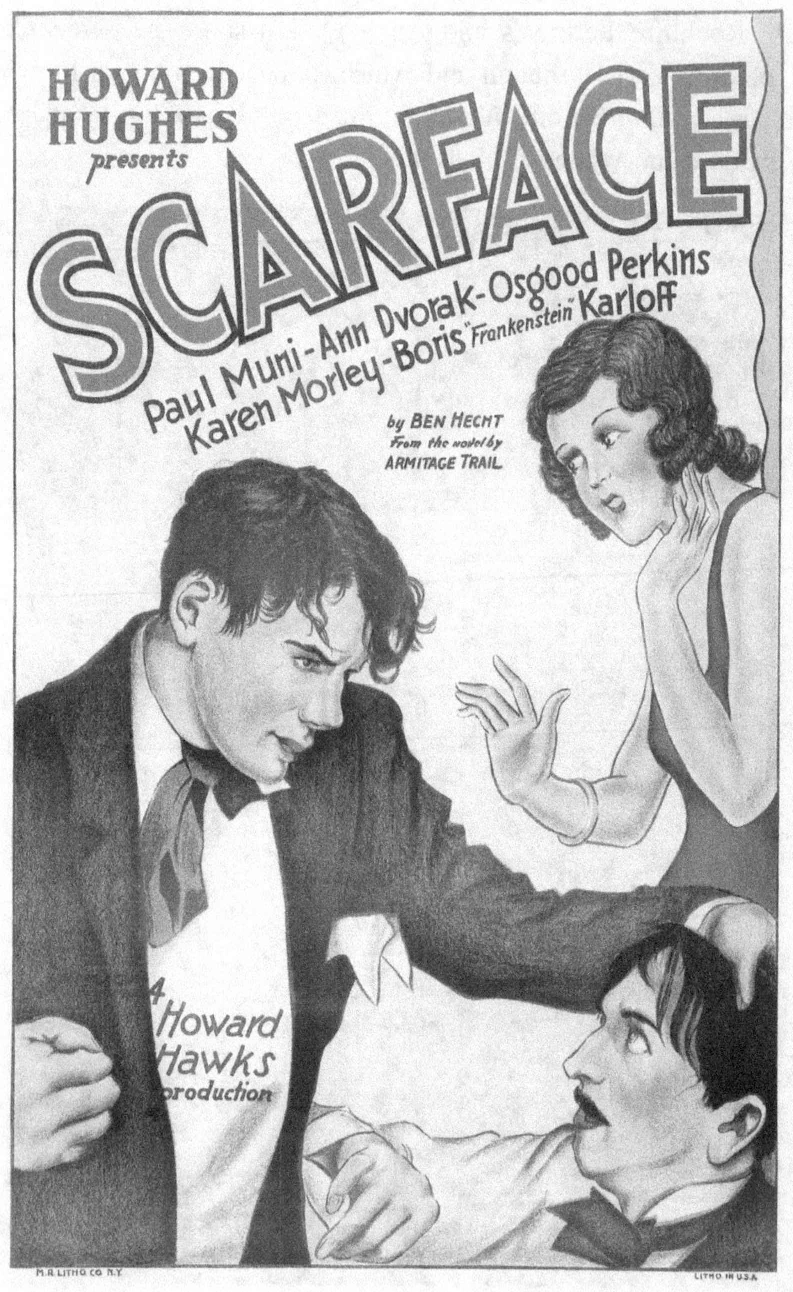

Theatrical poster for the release of the 1932 American film Scarface (1932).[xxi]

Lobby Card for the 1946 re-release of the film *Scarface* (1932), directed by Howard Hawks.[xxii]

Paul Muni in Scarface (1932) publicity still.[xxiii]

**Lobby card for the American pre-Code crime film Little Caesar
(1931).**[xxiv]

**"Style A" theatrical release poster of the 1931 American film Little
Caesar.**[xxv]

"Style B" theatrical release poster of the 1931 American film Little Caesar.[xxvi]

Poster for the 1931 film The Public Enemy.[xxvii]

The landmark gangster film *The Petrified Forest* was released in 1936, directed by Archie Mayo and based on Robert E. Sherwood's 1934 drama of the same name. It stars Leslie Howard, Bette Davis, and Humphrey Bogart. Notably, in the introduction of Abel Ferrara's

The Funeral, the character Johnny Tempio, played by Vincent Gallo, is shown watching the film in a New York cinema.

Screenshot of Humphrey Bogart from the trailer for the film The Petrified Forest.[xxviii]

"The screen version is still a play, but it's a turning point in the movie career of Humphrey Bogart, who had played the gangster's role on stage and then in a TV version with his wife (in the Bette Davis role)."- Emanuel Levy[24]

Photograph of the Broadway production of The Petrified Forest.[xxix]

---

24 *Emanuel Levy https://emanuellevy.com/review/petrifed-forest-the/*

The implementation of the Hays Code (also known as the Motion Picture Production Code) in the mid-1930s brought about substantial transformations in the film industry. This code required that any criminal behavior face the consequences and that all authority figures have respect.

"The Hays Code was this self-imposed industry set of guidelines for all the motion pictures that were released between 1934 and 1968," said Chelsey O'Brien. "The code prohibited profanity, suggestive nudity, graphic or realistic violence, sexual persuasions and rape."[25]

Gangster films became scarce in the following three decades. Then with the abolition of the Hays Code in the late 1960s, studios and filmmakers found themselves free to produce films dealing with subject matter that had previously been off-limits.[26]

1930s Motion Picture Production Code (Hays Code), cover of a paper copy.[xxx]

---

25 *https://www.acmi.net.au/stories-and-ideas/early-hollywood-and-hays-code/*
26 *Cortés, Carlos E. (1987). "Italian-Americans in Film: From Immigrants to Icons". MELUS. **14** (3/4): 117. doi:10.2307/467405. JSTOR 467405*

Thou Shalt Not, photograph created by Whitey Schafer (1902/3– 1951) in 1940 to protest the Hays Code. This image is in the public domain.[xxxi]

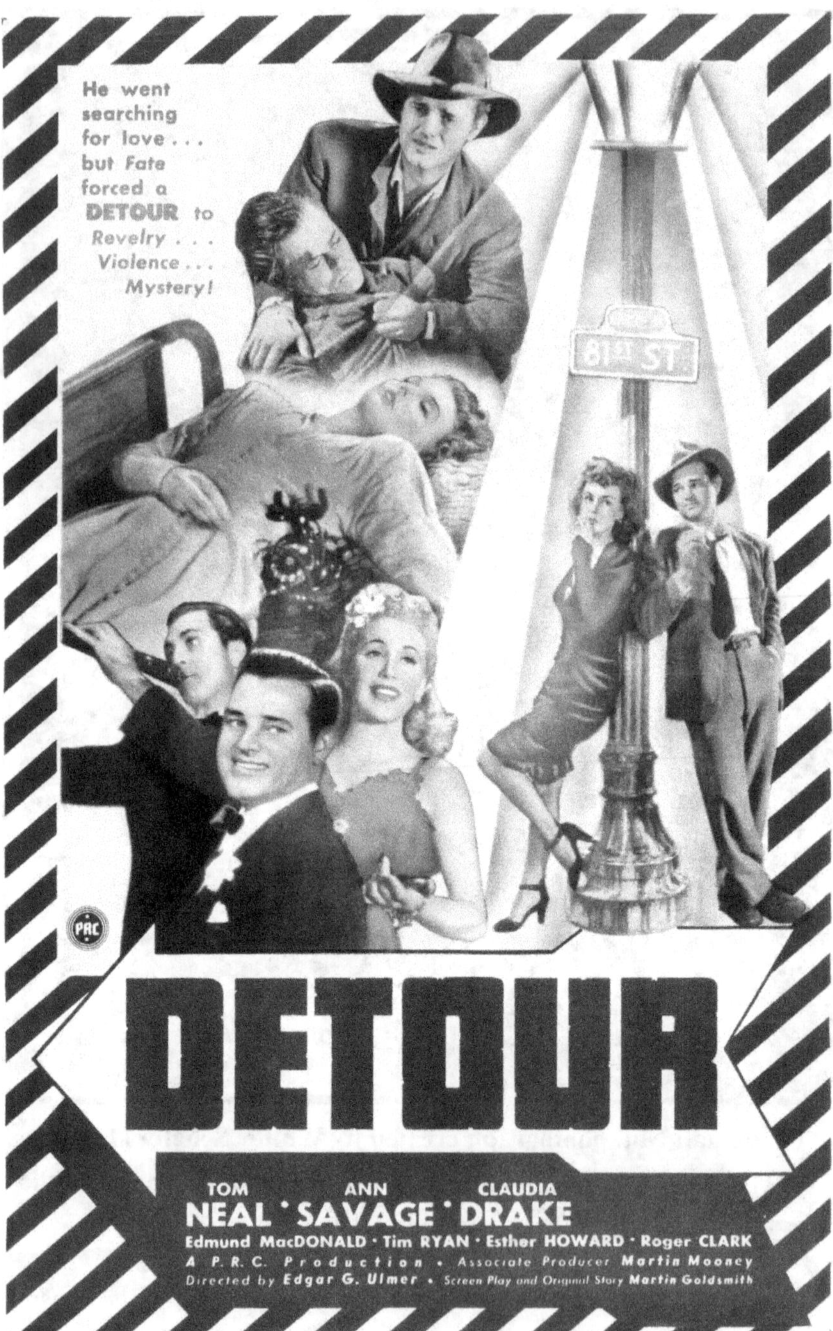

Poster for the 1945 film Detour.[xxxii]

Theatrical release poster of the 1950 American film Gun Crazy.[xxxiii]

Alternate Theatrical release poster of the 1950 American film Gun Crazy.[xxxiv]

"The codes of the time prevented Lewis from being explicit about the extent to which their fast-blooming romance is fueled by their mutual love of weaponry (Arthur Penn would rip off the covers in Bonnie and Clyde, which owes Gun Crazy a substantial debt), but when Cummins' six-gun dangles provocatively as she gasses up their jalopy, it's clear what really fills their collective tank."- Sam Adams: Philadelphia City Paper[27]

Film poster for the 1955 film *The Big Combo*.[xxxv]

27 *Sam Adams Philadelphia City Paper 2008-05-22 at the Wayback Machine. Philadelphia City Paper, film review.*

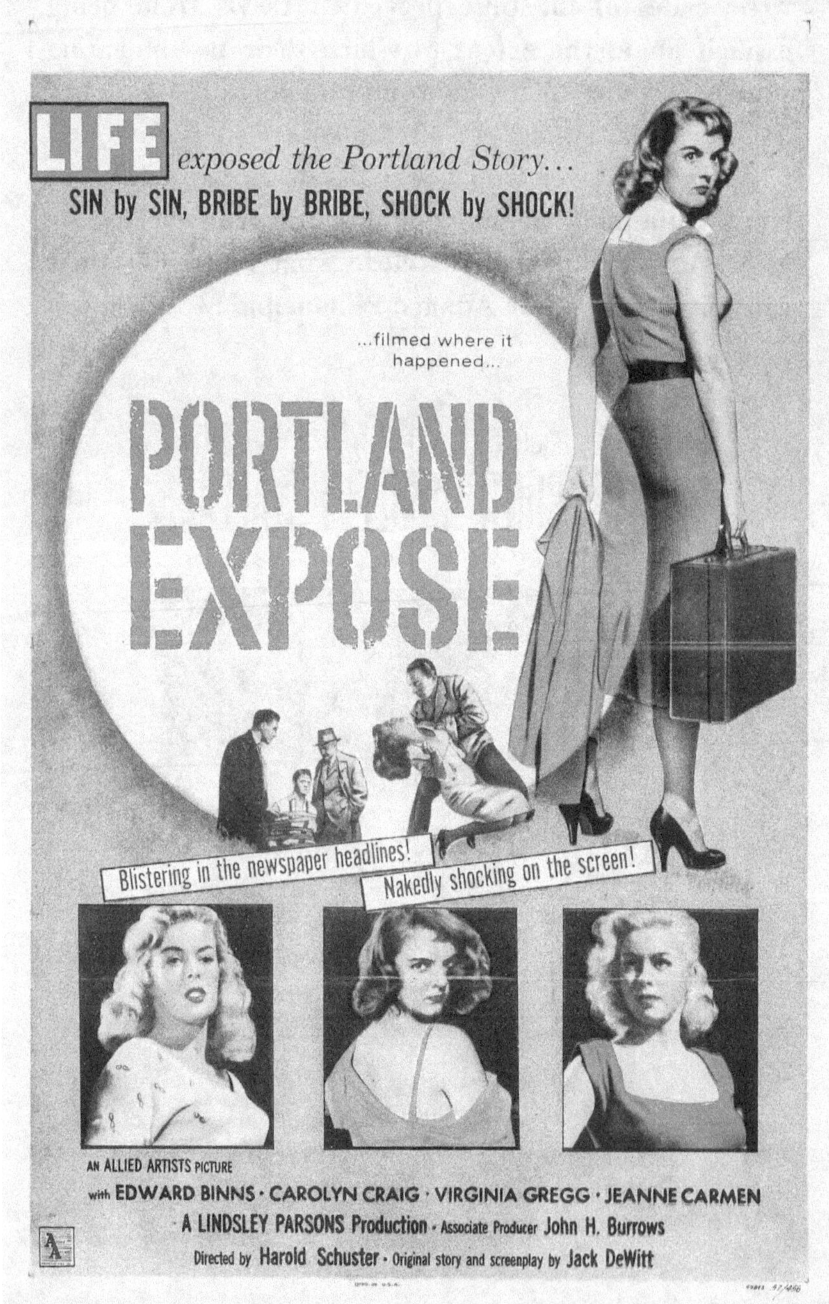

Poster for film Portland Exposé, 1957.[xxxvi]

Advertising poster for the film The Bonnie Parker Story (1958).[xxxvii]

"The Bonnie Parker Story is an obscure oddity that exists in the shadow of the far better known Bonnie and Clyde, but this little film is also able to stand on its own legs."-Bob Mastrangelo[28]

The American New Wave, commonly known as New Hollywood, was a movement in American film history that lasted from the mid-1960s to the early 1980s. During this period, a new generation of talented filmmakers made their mark on the industry. These directors brought a remarkable line-up of exceptional and influential films, including Martin Scorsese, Stanley Kubrick, Francis Ford Coppola, Robert Altman, Steven Spielberg, George Lucas, and Brian De Palma. A groundbreaking picture, Bonnie and Clyde was one of the pioneering films that emerged during the New Hollywood era. This movie aimed to present a romantic and comedic perspective on the violent gangster films of the 1930s, incorporating modern filmmaking techniques and giving it a fresh twist.[29] Critic Roger Ebert called the film "a milestone in the history of American movies, a work of truth and brilliance," stating, "It is also pitilessly cruel, filled with sympathy, nauseating, funny, heartbreaking, and astonishingly beautiful. If it does not seem that those words should be strung together, perhaps that is because movies do not very often reflect the full range of human life."[30]

---

28 *https://www.allmovie.com/movie/the-bonnie-parker-story-am56189*
29 *The Movies by Richard Griffith, Arthur Mayer, and Eileen Bowser. New York: Simon & Schuster, 1981 edition.*
30 *Roger Ebert (September 25, 1967). "Bonnie and Clyde"*

Bowie theater advertisement for the biographical neo-noir crime film, Bonnie and Clyde. 22 September 1967.[xxxviii]

Window card poster to promote showings of the 1967 film Bonnie and Clyde at college campuses.

"That was kind of the way with Bonnie Parker and Clyde Barrow. They didn't seem to be able to see their crimes in context. They killed all these people, and it was still a game for them, a lark. What we tried to do in the movie was put the humor and the violence in the same framework, to make a point about the social climate that produced the Barrow Gang."–Warren Beatty[31]

Francis Ford Coppola in 1976.40

In 1972, Francis Ford Coppola pioneered Italian-American mafia films with The Godfather, based on Mario Puzo's best-selling 1969 novel. The Godfather Part II followed in 1974. The epic story chronicles the Corleone family's generational transition from post-prohibition to post-war, their fratricidal intrigues, and their involvement in mid-century America's criminal underworld. The film was a massive hit, both critically and commercially. After

31 *Roger Ebert (December 14, 2012). https://www.rogerebert.com/interviews/ interview-with-warren-beatty*

stating in the audio commentary for Part II that he had covered the entire Corleone saga with the first two films, Francis Ford Coppola rejected numerous requests from Paramount to create a third installment for more than ten years. Nonetheless, due to extensive financial troubles resulting from the disappointing reception and commercial performance of One from the Heart (1982), he ultimately yielded and agreed to the persistent offer.[32]

The release date of The Godfather Part III was December 25, 1990. Francis Ford Coppola came back as the director for the full-length movie, collaborating with author Mario Puzo to write the screenplay. For the film's 30th anniversary, a recut titled The Godfather Coda: The Death of Michael Corleone received a limited theatrical release on December 4, 2020. This version includes changes to the beginning and the ending, and some re-edited scenes and musical cues. It has a runtime of 158 minutes.[33]

Coppola said the 2020 recut is the one he and Puzo originally envisioned, and that it "vindicates" its status in The Godfather trilogy, as well as his daughter Sofia's performance.[34]

Writing for IndieWire, David Ehrlich said, "But when it was announced that [Coppola] had inevitably assembled a new cut of his most famous cause célèbre and re-christened it with the title he'd always wanted for the film... he wasn't trying to make it 'better' so much as he was trying to shift its place in history and reframe the picture as less the third part of a flawed trilogy than the postscript of a legendary dyad."[35]

Between the 1970s and 1980s, there was a consistent release of films by film studios that focused on Italian-American gangsters and

---

32 *"DVD commentary featuring Francis Ford Coppola". The Godfather Part II DVD. 2005.*

33 *"Francis Ford Coppola Recutting 'Godfather: Part III' For 30th Anniversary"*

34 *Ryan Parker (December 3, 2020). "Francis Ford Coppola Says 'Godfather: Part III' Recut Vindicates Film, Daughter Sofia"*

35 *David Ehrlich (December 10, 2020). "How 'The Godfather Coda' Allows Francis Ford Coppola to Redefine His Biggest Disappointment"*

the Mafia. Once Upon a Time in America, a 1984 epic crime film directed by Italian filmmaker, Sergio Leone and starring Robert De Niro and James Woods, was a product of this trend. This film, based on Harry Grey's novel, The Hoods, marked Leone's final directorial work before his death five years later, it was also his first feature film in 13 years. Once Upon a Time in America is part of Leone's Once Upon a Time Trilogy, alongside Once Upon a Time in the West (1968) and Duck, You Sucker! (also known as A Fistful of Dynamite and Once Upon a Time...the Revolution, 1971). In his review of Brian De Palma's The Untouchables, Roger Ebert declared the original uncut version of Once Upon a Time in America to be the best film depicting the Prohibition era.[36]

James Woods, who regards it as Leone's greatest film, mentioned in the DVD documentary that a critic initially labeled the film as the worst of 1984. However, after watching the original version years later, the same critic praised it as the best film of the 1980s.[37]

Released in 1985, Prizzi's Honor is a dark comedy crime film directed by John Huston, starring Jack Nicholson and Kathleen Turner as two highly-skilled mob assassins who, after falling in love, are hired to kill each other. The screenplay, co-written by Richard Condon, is based on his 1982 novel of the same name. The film received eight nominations at the 58th Academy Awards, including Best Picture, Best Director, Best Actor, and Best Adapted Screenplay, with Anjelica Huston winning Best Supporting Actress. The film also won four Golden Globe Awards, including Best Actor – Motion Picture Musical or Comedy and Best Actress – Motion Picture Comedy or Musical for Nicholson and Turner, respectively.

"This John Huston picture has a ripe and daring comic tone. It revels voluptuously in the murderous finagling of

---

36 *Roger Ebert (3 June 1987). "The Untouchables (1987)" https://www. rogerebert.com/reviews/the-untouchables-1987*

37 *Once Upon a Time: Sergio Leone (Documentary) (in English and Italian). CreaTVty, Westbrook. 8 January 2001.*

the members of a Brooklyn Mafia family, and rejoices in their scams. It's like The Godfather acted out by The Munsters. Jack Nicholson's average-guyness as Charley, the clan's enforcer, is the film's touchstone: this is a baroque comedy about people who behave in ordinary ways in grotesque circumstances, and it has the juice of everyday family craziness in it."- Pauline Kael[38]

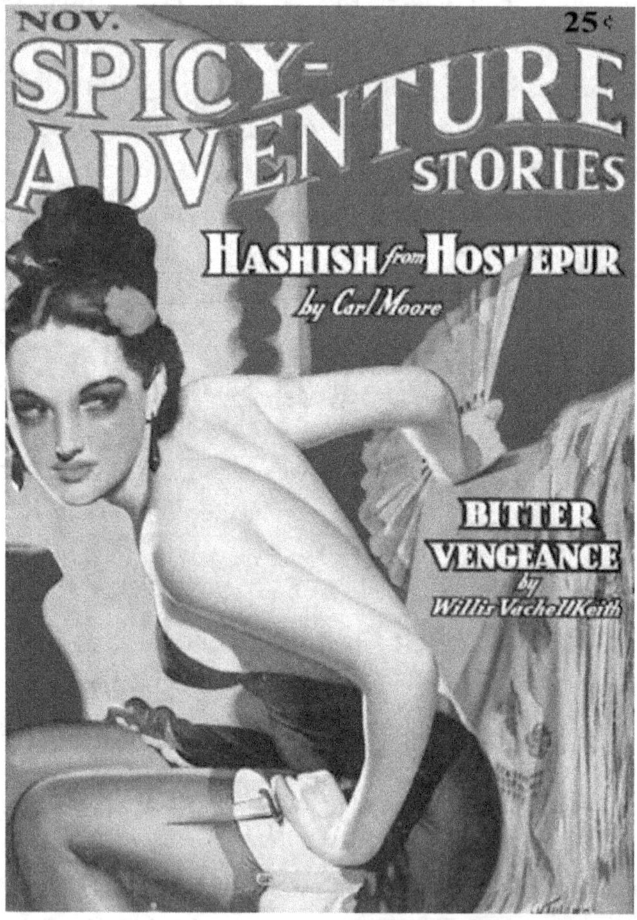

The gangster's moll is the female companion of a male professional criminal. Femme fatales were standard fare in hardboiled crime stories in 1930s pulp fiction.[xli]

---

38 *Pauline Kael (New Yorker) https://scrapsfromtheloft.com/movies/prizzis-honor-pauline-kael/*

During the 1990s, numerous mob films gained critical acclaim, with many being inspired by actual crimes and criminals. Notably, Goodfellas, directed by Martin Scorsese, stood out among the gangster films of the decade. Ray Liotta portrayed Henry Hill, an associate of the Lucchese crime family, while Robert De Niro, and Joe Pesci also had prominent roles. Pesci's performance ultimately earned him an Academy Award for Best Actor in a Supporting Role. With a total of six Academy Award nominations, including Best Picture and Best Director, the film firmly established itself as one of the most highly praised crime films ever made.

Chicago Sun-Times, Roger Ebert gave the film a full four stars and wrote, "No finer film has ever been made about organized crime – not even The Godfather."[39]

State of Grace is a film directed by Phil Joanou, starring Sean Penn, Ed Harris, Gary Oldman, Robin Wright, John Turturro, and John C. Reilly. Although it did not achieve commercial success due to being released alongside Martin Scorsese's Goodfellas, it was well-received by most critics. The film was shot on location in New York City and draws inspiration from the real-life "Hell's Kitchen" gang known as the Westies. The Westies were an Irish American organized crime gang based in New York City. They were known for engaging in racketeering, drug trafficking, and contract killing. They were aligned with the Italian-American Mafia and were active in the "Hell's Kitchen" neighborhood of Manhattan.[40]

Chuck O'Leary gave the film a full five stars and wrote, "A gritty, intense and explosive Irish gangster drama that's second only to Scorsese's GoodFellas as the best film of 1990."[41]

---

39 *"GoodFellas". Chicago Sun-Times. (September 2,1990). https://www.rogerebert.com/reviews/goodfellas-1990*

40 *English, T. J. The Westies: Inside New York's Irish Mob (1991); St. Martins Press; ISBN 0312362846/ISBN 978-0312362843.*

41 *Chuck O'Leary, Fantastica Daily. (October 10, 2005).*

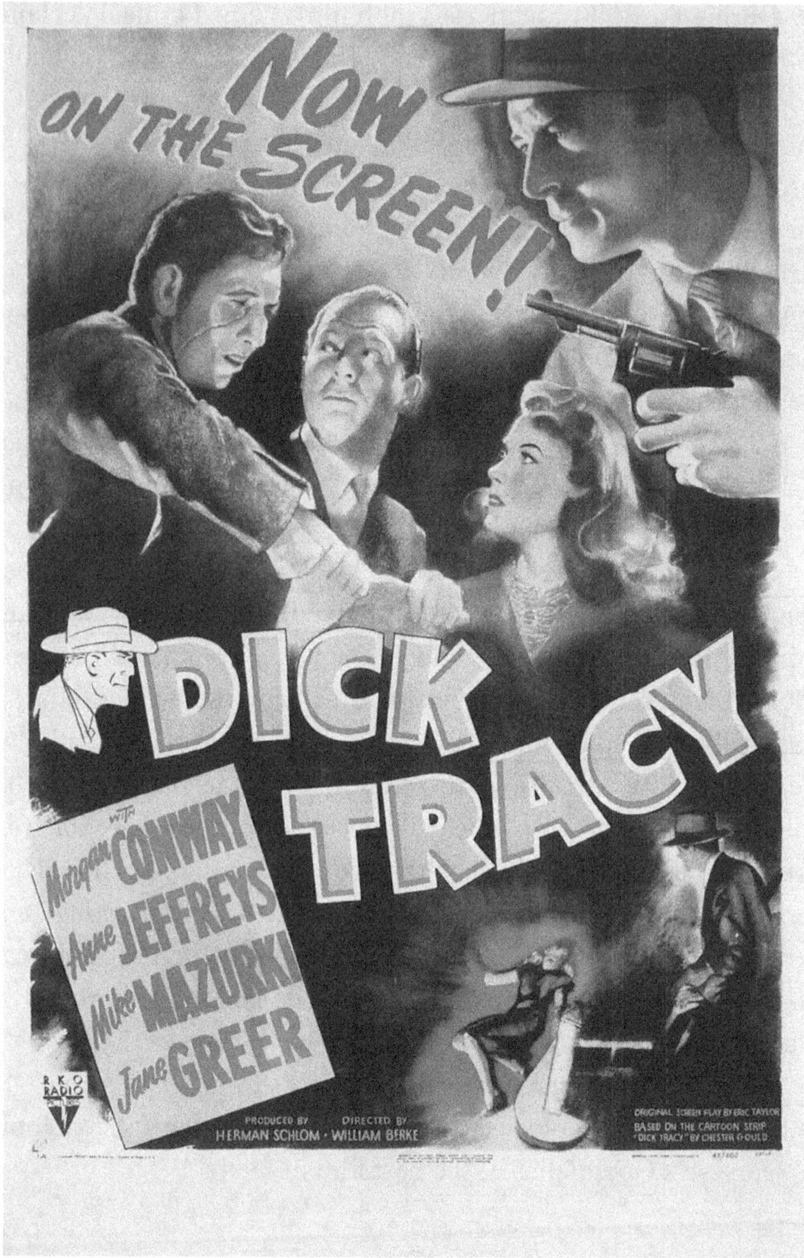

Poster from Dick Tracy (1945) The film is the first of four installment of the Dick Tracy film series, released by RKO Radio Pictures.[xlii]

The 1930s comic strip Dick Tracy, created by Chester Gould, is about a detective relentlessly pursuing criminal. The character of

Dick Tracy has been featured in the following films: Dick Tracy (1945), Dick Tracy vs. Cueball (1946), Dick Tracy's Dilemma (1947), Dick Tracy Meets Gruesome (1947), and in 1990's Dick Tracy, which Warren Beatty produced, directed, and starred in. The supporting cast includes Al Pacino, Madonna, Glenne Headly, and Charlie Korsmo, with appearances by Dustin Hoffman, James Keane, Charles Durning, William Forsythe, Seymour Cassel, Mandy Patinkin, Catherine O'Hara, Ed O'Ross, James Caan, James Tolkan, R. G. Armstrong, and Dick Van Dyke. The film was nominated for seven Academy Awards, winning three for Best Original Song, Best Makeup, and Best Art Direction.

"This is a larger-than-life comic strip come-to-life, and its success comes from Warren Beatty making all the right moves to make the ultimate Dick Tracy movie."- Aaron Neuwirth[42]

Shel Dorf with Warren Beatty on the set of the 1990 Dick Tracy movie. Shel Dorf (July 5, 1933 - November 3, 2009) was a primary founder of the San Diego Comic Con, today known as Comic Con International. Photo Credit: Alan Light.

42 *Aaron Neuwirth, We Live Entertainment. https://weliveentertainment.com/ welivefilm/in-house-reviews-the-high-note-the-vast-of-night-the-lovebirds-more/*

   The Greatest Gangster Movie You've Never Seen

Shel Dorf, the founder of San Diego Comic Con International, with Warren Beatty on the set of the 1990 Dick Tracy movie. Photo Credit: Alan Light.

Shel Dorf (1933-2009), the founder of San Diego Comic Con International, with Warren Beatty on the set of the 1990 Dick Tracy movie. Photo Credit: Alan Light.

Warren Beatty Photo taken at the 62nd Academy Awards 3/26/90.
Photo Credit: Alan Light.

Bugsy is a 1991 biographical crime drama film based on the life of American mobster Benjamin 'Bugsy' Siegel and his affair with starlet Virginia Hill. Directed by Barry Levinson and written by James Toback, the film stars Warren Beatty, Annette Bening, Harvey Keitel, Ben Kingsley, Elliott Gould, Bebe Neuwirth, and Joe Mantegna. It received ten nominations at the 64th Academy Awards and won two: Best Art Direction and Best Costume Design. The film also won the Golden Globe Award for Best Motion Picture - Drama.

"Bugsy perpetuates the gangster mystique in American mythology: It encourages the audiences' voyeurism of a deviant world full of frills, thrills, and glamour. But it also highlights better than other films the contradictions inherent in such lifestyle. Siegel is a charismatic, larger-than-life gangster, part murderer, part visionary."-Emanuel Levy[43]

---

43 *Emanuel Levy, EmanuelLevy.Com (December 24, 2005). https://emanuellevy.com/review/bugsy-2/*

"Warren Beatty delivers some of his best acting in years as Bugsy Siegel, the gangster responsible for the inception of Las Vegas as we now know it."- Jonathan Rosenbaum: Chicago Reader[44]

The crime genre film Reservoir Dogs marks Quentin Tarantino's directorial debut in 1992. The movie boasts an exceptional cast, including Harvey Keitel, Tim Roth, Chris Penn, Steve Buscemi, Lawrence Tierney, Michael Madsen, Quentin Tarantino himself, and Edward Bunker. The gripping plot revolves around a gang of diamond thieves whose plans take an unexpected and disastrous turn when they attempt to rob a jewelry store. Tarantino himself has said that Reservoir Dogs was influenced by Stanley Kubrick's 1956 film noir The Killing: "I didn't go out of my way to do a rip-off of The Killing, but I did think of it as my 'Killing', my take on that kind of heist movie."[45]

Caroline Jewers called Reservoir Dogs a "feudal epic" and paralleled the color pseudonyms to color names of medieval knights.[46]

Released in 1993 A Bronx Tale is the directorial debut of actor Robert De Niro, produced by Jane Rosenthal and adapted from Chazz Palminteri's 1989 play of the same name. In 1990, De Niro met with Palminteri in his dressing room after watching a performance of the one-man stage show "A Bronx Tale". De Niro told Palminteri, "This is one of the greatest one-man shows I've ever seen, if not the greatest ... This is a movie, this is an incredible movie."[47]

---

44 *Jonathan Rosenbaum, Chicago Reader (October 26,1991). https:// chicagoreader.com/film/bugsy/*

45 *John Hartl (October 29, 1992). "'Dogs' Gets Walkouts and Raves". The Seattle Times. pp. Arts, Entertainment, page F5.*

46 *Caroline Jewer, (2000). "Heroes and Heroin: From True Romance to Pulp Fiction". The Journal of Popular Culture. 33 (4): 39–61, 45–46. doi:10.1111/ j.0022-3840.2000.3304_39.x*

47 *Ryan Vlastelica (March 2, 2016). "Chazz Palminteri on A Bronx Tale, Keyser Söze, and Stallone's career advice"*

Returning to the genre Pacino and De Palma teamed up again in 1993 for Carlito's Way, a film that served as a reunion for the duo after their successful collaboration on Scarface in 1983. The movie follows the journey of a former gangster who is released from prison and is determined to change his life for the better. The story is based on Judge Edwin Torres' novels Carlito's Way and After Hours, published in 1975 and 1979 respectively, Alongside Pacino, the cast includes Sean Penn, Penelope Ann Miller, Luis Guzman, John Leguizamo, Jorge Porcel, Joseph Siravo, and Viggo Mortensen.

Directed and written by Michael Mann, the film Heat (1995) is a noteworthy collaboration between legendary actors De Niro and Pacino, marking their second project together since The Godfather Part II. With a string of acclaimed performances under their belts, both actors' involvement in the film was heavily emphasized during its promotion. Inspired by the real-life tale of Neil McCauley, a cunning ex-Alcatraz prisoner pursued by Detective Chuck Adamson in 1964, Heat captures the essence of these iconic figures in the crime genre.

In the book "Michael Mann: Crime Auteur" by Steven Rybin the director talked about the connection between cop and criminal. *"Chuck had respected the guy's professionalism — he was a really good thief, which is exciting to a detective, and he tried to keep any risks to a minimum — but at the same time he was a cold-blooded sociopath who'd kill you as soon as look at you — if necessary..."*[48]

Chuck Adamson went on to have a career as a television and film producer, and he died in 2008 at age 71.[49] Mann's 2009 film Public Enemies is dedicated to Adamson's memory.

Michael Mann's Heat ranks right up there with the best of the crime genre from Rififi to The Godfather. In fact, it is the single greatest Los Angeles crime epic of all time.[50]

---

48 *Michael Mann: Crime Auteur by Steven Rybin ISBN-13: 978-0810890831*

49 *Chuck Adamson". Las Vegas Review-Journal. (March 2, 2008).*

50 *Wael Khairy RogerEbert.com https://www.rogerebert.com/far-flung-correspondents/crime-in-the-emptiness-of-los-angeles*

In 1995, following their collaboration on Goodfellas, Martin Scorsese, Robert De Niro, Joe Pesci, and screenwriter Nicholas Pileggi teamed up again to make Casino, based on Pileggi's nonfiction book "Casino: Love and Honor in Las Vegas." The film is inspired by the true story of Frank Rosenthal, an associate of the Chicago Outfit who ran multiple casinos in Las Vegas during the 1970s and 1980s. For the film, the real names of the characters Rosenthal and Tony Spilotro were changed to Ace Rothstein and Nicky Santoro, portrayed by Robert De Niro and Joe Pesci, respectively. Sharon Stone, playing Rothstein's wife, Ginger (based on Geri McGee), was nominated for the Academy Award for Best Actress and won the Golden Globe Award for Best Actress in a Motion Picture – Drama.

Gotti is a 1996 crime drama television film directed by Robert Harmon and written by Steve Shagan. It is partly based on the 1996 non-fiction book "Gotti: Rise and Fall" by Jerry Capeci and Gene Mustain. The film stars Armand Assante in the title role as the infamous Gambino crime family boss John Gotti, alongside William Forsythe and Anthony Quinn. Howard Rosenberg of the *Los Angeles Times* called it "one of the better mob movies of the decade, and surely the best gangster portrait ever made primarily for television".[51]

Donnie Brasco is a crime drama film that was released in 1997, directed by Mike Newell. The film stars Al Pacino and Johnny Depp in the lead roles, with supporting performances by Michael Madsen, Bruno Kirby, James Russo, and Anne Heche. The story is loosely based on the real-life experience of FBI agent Joe Pistone (played by Depp), who infiltrated the Bonanno crime family in New York City during the 1970s under the name Donnie Brasco, a jewel thief from Vero Beach, Florida. The screenplay was written by Paul Attanasio and is based on the book Donnie Brasco: "My Undercover Life in the Mafia," which was co-written by Joseph D. Pistone and Richard Woodley and published in 1988. The film was nominated

---

51 *Howard Rosenberg (1996-08-17). "Sincerely Sinister". Los Angeles Times.*

for an Academy Award for Best Adapted Screenplay. *Entertainment Weekly* called the film "wonderfully dense, clever, and moving gangland thriller," and gave it an A−, also praising Paul Attanasio's screenplay as "a rich, satisfying gumbo of back stabbing, shady business maneuvers, and mayhem."[52]

In 1999, the HBO series The Sopranos, created by David Chase, forever changed the landscape of television. The series centers on Tony Soprano (James Gandolfini), a New Jersey-based Italian-American mobster who struggles to balance his family life with his role as the leader of a criminal organization. His internal conflicts are reluctantly explored during therapy sessions with psychiatrist Jennifer Melfi (Lorraine Bracco). The series received numerous accolades, including Peabody Awards for its first two seasons, 21 Primetime Emmy Awards, and five Golden Globe Awards. In 2013, the Writers Guild of America named The Sopranos the best-written TV series of all time.[53] *TV Guide* also ranked it the greatest television series of all time.[54] In both 2016 and 2022, the series topped *Rolling Stone*'s list of the 100 greatest TV shows of all time.[55][56]

In 2021, The Many Saints of Newark was released as a prequel to David Chase's HBO series The Sopranos. Directed by Alan Taylor and produced by David Chase and Lawrence Konner, the film centers on the young future mafia boss Tony Soprano, set against the backdrop of the 1967 Newark riots.[57]

---

52 *Owen Gleiberman (March 17, 1997). "Rev. of Donnie Brasco (1997)". Entertainment Weekly.*

53 *"'101 Best Written TV Series Of All Time' From WGA/TV Guide: Complete List". Deadline. June 2, 2013.*

54 *Matt Fretts, Bruce; Roush (December 23, 2013). "TV Guide Magazine's 60 Best Series of All Time".*

55 *Rob Sheffield (September 21, 2016). "100 Greatest TV Shows of All Time".*

56 *Alan Sepinwall (September 26, 2022). "The 100 Greatest TV Shows of All Time".*

57 *Mike Jr. Flemming (January 7, 2019). "'The Sopranos' Creator David Chase Offers Glimpses Of Prequel Movie As Groundbreaking HBO Series Turns 20". https://deadline.com/2019/01/the-sopranos-david-chase-20th*

"I was against [the movie] for a long time and I'm still very worried about it, but I became interested in Newark, where my parents came from, and where the riots took place...I was living in suburban New Jersey at the time that happened, and my girlfriend was working in downtown Newark. I was just interested in the whole Newark riot thing. I started thinking about those events and organized crime, and I just got interested in mixing those two elements."- David Chase[58]

Released in 2002, Road to Perdition was directed by Sam Mendes. It was written by David Self, based on the graphic novel series of the same name by Max Allan Collins and Richard Piers Rayner. The film stars Tom Hanks, Paul Newman (in his final live-action theatrical role), Jude Law, Jennifer Jason Leigh, Stanley Tucci, Daniel Craig, and Tyler Hoechlin in his film debut. Set in 1931 during the Great Depression, the story revolves around fathers, sons, and gangsters. The film was nominated for Best Supporting Actor for Newman, Best Original Score, Best Sound Editing, Best Sound Mixing, and Best Art Direction. Conrad Hall was posthumously awarded the Oscar for Best Cinematography.[59]

"Gangsters. Parents. Children. Honor. 'Road to Perdition' is all this and more, perhaps too perfect or too

---

-anniversary-prequel-film-tony-soprano-the-many-saints-of-newark-1202530544/

58 *Mike Jr.Flemming (January 7, 2019). "'The Sopranos' Creator David Chase Offers Glimpses Of Prequel Movie As Groundbreaking HBO Series Turns 20".   https://deadline.com/2019/01/the-sopranos-david-chase-20th-anniversary-prequel-film-tony-soprano-the-many-saints-of-newark-1202530544/*

59 *"Winners: Big upsets". Detroit Free Press. 24 March 2003. p. 21. Newspapers. com*

calculated, but with great cinema in it."- Alberto Abuín: Espinof[60]

"...it's a modern throwback to the classic gangster movie, set in the depths of the Depression in 1930s America, and Mendes pays great attention to the imagery of the screen adaptation."- Sean Axmaker: Stream on Demand[61]

Directed by Michael Mann, who co-wrote and produced Public Enemies, the film is a biographical crime drama film released in 2009. It is Based on the book: "Public Enemies: America's Greatest Crime Wave and the Birth of the FBI, 1933–34" by Bryan Burrough. The film depicts the notorious bank robber John Dillinger, played by Johnny Depp, as he is pursued by FBI agent Melvin Purvis, portrayed by Christian Bale. It also explores Dillinger's relationship with Billie Frechette played by Marion Cotillard, as well as Purvis' pursuit of Dillinger's associates and fellow criminals: John "Red" Hamilton (Jason Clarke), Homer Van Meter (Stephen Dorff), Harry Pierpont (David Wenham), and Baby Face Nelson (Stephen Graham). Depp described John Dillinger as a "...man of the people... There is a Robin Hood edge to John Dillinger."[62] and "that era's rock and roll star. He was a very charismatic man and he lived the way he wanted to and didn't compromise."[63]

---

60 *https://www.espinof.com/criticas/paul-newman-camino-a-la-perdicion-de-sam-mendes*

61 *https://streamondemandathome.com/road-to-perdition-tom-hanks-dvd-blu-ray-dvd/*

62 *Dean Reynolds; On the trail of John Dillinger, CBS News. https://www.cbsnews.com/news/on-the-trail-of-john-dillinger/*

63 *John Hiscock, (June 25, 2009). "Johnny Depp interview for Public Enemies". https://www.telegraph.co.uk/culture/film/starsandstories/5635464/Johnny-Depp-interview-for-Public-Enemies.html*

"The desperate times in which we suddenly find ourselves ... make Public Enemies seem especially timely."- Andrew Sarris: Film Comment Magazine[64]

In 2006, Martin Scorsese released The Departed, his American remake of Infernal Affairs, a Hong Kong film. The Departed was also loosely based on the Whitey Bulger story and Boston's Winter Hill Gang, which Bulger led. Jack Nicholson's character, Frank Costello, was based on Whitey Bulger. The film earned Scorsese an Academy Award for Best Director and won the Academy Award for Best Picture.

The Departed received one award for Best Director (Martin Scorsese) and was nominated for five other awards, including Best Picture, Best Actor (Leonardo DiCaprio), Best Supporting Actor (Jack Nicholson, Mark Wahlberg), and Best Screenplay (William Monahan).

At the 79th Academy Awards on February 25, 2007, The Departed won four Academy Awards: Best Picture (Graham King), Best Director (Martin Scorsese), Best Film Editing (Thelma Schoonmaker), and Best Adapted Screenplay (William Monahan). Mark Wahlberg was also nominated for Best Supporting Actor for his performance.

"[The Departed] showcases Scorsese's trademark themes of sin, betrayal and redemption. It's a carefully calibrated and detailed film that takes its time establishing the characters' complex histories."- Jeff Meyers: Metro Times (Detroit, MI)[65]

American Gangster, released in 2007, is a biographical crime film directed and produced by Ridley Scott and written by Steven

64 *Andrew Sarris, Film Comment Magazine: https://leitch.tumblr.com/ post/162964597/movie-roundup-ive-been-spending-my-summer*

65 *Jeff Meyers: Metro Times (Detroit, MI) http://www2.metrotimes.com/archives/ review.asp?rid=22762*

Zaillian. The film is based on the criminal career of Frank Lucas, a gangster from La Grange, North Carolina, who smuggled heroin into the United States on American service planes returning from the Vietnam War, before being detained by a task force led by Newark Detective Richie Roberts. The film stars Denzel Washington and Russell Crowe. American Gangster was nominated for twenty-one awards, including two Oscar nominations for Best Art Direction and Best Supporting Actress for Ruby Dee, who also won a Screen Actors Guild Award for Outstanding Performance by a Female Actor in a Supporting Role.

"When I met Frank, I really understood what I saw as the arc of the character. He wears nice clothes and drives fancy cars and all that, so if that means glorifying it I guess that's the case. But for me I was looking at the arc of the character, and he don't look that glorious right now."- Denzel Washington discussing the arc of Frank Lucas[66]

The Irishman marks the ninth collaboration between Scorsese and De Niro, in addition to Martin Scorsese's fifth collaboration with Harvey Keitel, his fourth with Joe Pesci, his first with Al Pacino, the fourth collaboration between Pacino and De Niro, and the first collaboration between Pacino and Pesci. Released in 2019, The Irishman is an American epic gangster film directed and produced by Martin Scorsese from a screenplay by Steven Zaillian, based on the 2004 book "I Heard You Paint Houses" by Charles Brandt. It stars Robert De Niro, Al Pacino, and Joe Pesci, with Ray Romano, Bobby Cannavale, Anna Paquin, Stephen Graham, Stephanie Kurtzuba, Jesse Plemons, and Harvey Keitel in supporting roles. The film follows Frank Sheeran (De Niro), a truck driver who

---

66 *Tony Jr. Rivetti (October 29, 2006). "Gross National Product: The Heroin Trade's New Face". The New York Times. https://www.nytimes.com/2006/10/29/ movies/29lela.html*

becomes a hitman involved with mobster Russell Bufalino (Pesci) and his crime family before later working for the powerful Teamster Jimmy Hoffa (Pacino). The Irishman received 10 Academy Award nominations, including Best Picture, Best Director, Best Supporting Actor for both Al Pacino and Joe Pesci, Best Adapted Screenplay, Best Production Design, Best Cinematography, Best Costume Design, Best Film Editing, and Best Visual Effects. However, it did not win in any category. The film was also nominated for five awards at the 77th Golden Globe Awards, including Best Motion Picture – Drama.

With all the examples above in the genre, it should help unlock both the history and appeal of the gangster genre, a genre that has had a profound effect on audiences and the zeitgeist. From Italian-made gangster films, British gangster films, Japan and the Yakuza, Indian cinema, Hong Kong, Russia, to comedies and parodies, this genre has reached an international level and continues to pervade and make a huge impact.

Chapter 8

A Gem of the Gangster Genre: Abel Ferrara's The Funeral

The Funeral, released in 1996, stands as a hidden gem within the gangster genre, offering a profound and gritty exploration of crime, family, and redemption. Starring Christopher Walken, Annabella Sciorra, Chris Penn, Isabella Rossellini, Benicio del Toro, Vincent Gallo and Gretchen Mol. Chris Penn won the Volpi Cup for Best Supporting Actor at the 1996 Venice Film Festival for his performance. The film received five Independent Spirit Awards nominations, including Best Film, Best Director, Best Actor, Best Screenplay and Best Cinematography.[67] Set against the backdrop of 1930s New York City, the film follows the tumultuous journey of three brothers as they navigate the treacherous waters of organized crime and personal tragedy. The Funeral distinguishes itself from other gangster films through its nuanced exploration of complex characters, its atmospheric cinematography by Ken Kelsch, and its evocative production design. One of the most striking aspects of The Funeral is its exploration of themes such as family, loyalty, and the quest for redemption. The film offers a nuanced portrayal of the Tempio family, depicting the complex dynamics between the brothers. Each character is richly developed, with their own motivations, conflicts, and moral complexities. From Johnny's brooding intensity to Chez's simmering rage to Ray's quiet introspection, the performances by Christopher Walken, Chris Penn, and Vincent Gallo bring depth and authenticity to their respective roles. These performances anchor the film's exploration of themes

---

67 *https://www.filmaffinity.com/en/award-edition-movie.php?edition-id=spirit_1997&movie-id=392855*

such as the bonds of family, the struggle for power, and the quest for redemption in a world defined by violence and corruption. Ken Kelsch's cinematography in The Funeral is equally mesmerizing, capturing the gritty atmosphere of 1930s New York City with haunting beauty. Kelsch employs the lighting and atmospheric framing to evoke a sense of foreboding and existential dread, immersing viewers in the dark and shadowy world of organized crime. The film's visual aesthetic serves as a powerful complement to its thematic exploration of moral ambiguity and existential despair, enhancing the emotional impact of key moments and heightening the tension between the characters. In addition to its performances and cinematography, The Funeral also features evocative production design that transports viewers to the bygone era of 1930s New York City. From the dimly-lit speakeasies to the opulent housing of the Tempio family, the film's production design creates a richly textured and immersive world that feels authentic and lived-in. The attention to detail in the costumes, set design, and props adds depth and authenticity to the film's portrayal of the Prohibition era, enhancing the overall sense of immersion and realism. Despite its critical acclaim and artistic merit, The Funeral remains relatively unknown compared to other gangster films of its time. However, its status as a hidden gem within the genre only adds to its allure and mystique, inviting viewers to discover its brilliance for themselves. With its complex characters, atmospheric cinematography, and evocative production design, The Funeral stands as a testament to Abel Ferrara's skill as a filmmaker and his ability to push the boundaries of cinematic storytelling. It is a film that deserves to be seen and appreciated by a wider audience, not only for its contributions to the gangster genre but also for its profound exploration of the human condition in all its complexity and ambiguity.

Chapter 9

The Tempio Family and The Roles of Women in The Funeral

In most gangster films, the focus is often on men and their violent lives. Women are usually background characters, serving as wives, mothers, or love interests without much influence on the plot. But in The Funeral, Abel Ferrara does something different. He places the women in the Tempio family at the heart of the story, showing how their emotions, opinions, and actions shape much of the film's drama. This chapter looks closely at how Ferrara gives Clara and Jean Tempio, the main women in the film, crucial roles that add depth to the story.

Clara Tempio: The Heart of the Family

Clara, played by Isabella Rossellini, is married to Chez (Chris Penn), one of the three Tempio brothers. Chez is grieving the death of his younger brother Johnny, and like his older brother Ray (Christopher Walken), he wants revenge. But unlike Chez, Clara doesn't think violence will solve anything. She's not just the stereotypical gangster's wife who stands by and watches as her husband destroys everything. Instead, Clara actively tries to change her husband's mind and protect their family from more harm.

In the film, Clara often speaks up, trying to reason with Chez. She's clear in her opposition to his violent tendencies, showing frustration with how deeply he's pulled into the world of crime. Even though she loves her husband, Clara is not afraid to tell him when she thinks he's wrong. This brings a real human connection to the story—Clara is not just an ornament to Chez's life, but a person with her own thoughts and feelings. Her attempts to pull him away from violence come from a deep love for him and a desire to protect their future together.

Through Clara, Ferrara highlights the struggles of women who are tied to men involved in crime. She doesn't approve of Chez's choices, but she also doesn't walk away from him. Instead, Clara remains by his side, hoping he will change. Her role in the film isn't passive—she is actively involved in the drama, often clashing with Chez as she tries to steer him in a better direction. This is a big difference from many other gangster films where the women are either silent or complicit in their husband's crimes. Clara stands out as a moral voice in a world filled with chaos.

Jean Tempio: The Silent Observer

Jean Tempio, played by Annabella Sciorra, is Ray's wife. While she doesn't speak up as much as Clara, her presence is just as important. Jean is quiet and observant, watching as Ray descends deeper into a spiral of revenge. Ray is cold and calculating, and it's clear that his choices weigh heavily on Jean. Though she doesn't confront Ray directly like Clara does with Chez, Jean's disapproval is always present. She serves as a silent reminder of the emotional damage that comes with living a life of crime.

One of the more subtle elements of Jean's role is how she responds to the violence around her. While she's not directly involved in the criminal activities, Jean's sadness and frustration can be felt throughout the film. She often looks on as Ray makes dangerous decisions, her face showing the toll it takes on her. Jean's silence says more than words ever could. Ferrara uses Jean's quiet disapproval to show the internal suffering of a woman who loves a man but despises the life he leads.

Jean's character represents many women who find themselves tied to men in the criminal underworld. She doesn't have the power to change Ray's decisions, but she also doesn't fully accept them. Jean seems to have resigned herself to the fact that Ray will never change, and this gives her character a deep sadness. While Clara fights to change Chez, Jean stands as a witness to Ray's self-destruction. Her emotional distance from Ray is a key part of the film, as it shows how crime can tear apart not only families but also the emotional bonds between people.

Women's Emotional Strength in The Funeral

One of the key things Ferrara does with these two women is show how their emotional strength contrasts with the men's emotional weaknesses. Chez and Ray are consumed by their need for revenge. Their grief over Johnny's death pushes them into a spiral of violence, and they are unable to process their emotions in a healthy way. They see violence as the only solution, and this leads them down a path of destruction. In contrast, Clara and Jean deal with their grief in a much more reflective and thoughtful manner. They don't rush to revenge; instead, they question the point of it all.

Clara's emotional strength comes from her deep understanding of what violence can do to a person. She knows that revenge won't bring Johnny back, and she tries to make Chez see this too. But Chez, blinded by his grief and anger, can't hear her. This creates a tragic tension in the film. Clara is right, but she can't stop Chez from doing what he thinks he needs to do. Her emotional intelligence stands in stark contrast to Chez's emotional immaturity. While Chez is driven by his pain, Clara tries to heal through understanding and compassion.

Jean's emotional strength is quieter, but just as powerful. She doesn't fight Ray's decisions, but she doesn't accept them either. Instead, she stays emotionally distant from him, knowing that nothing she says or does will change his course. Jean's emotional strength lies in her ability to remain grounded, even as Ray loses himself in his quest for revenge. She may not have the power to stop him, but she doesn't let herself be consumed by his actions. This makes her a strong presence in the film, even though she doesn't play an active role in the drama.

Challenging the Gender Norms of Gangster Films

Ferrara's decision to give Clara and Jean such prominent roles in The Funeral is unusual for a gangster film. In many films of this genre, women are secondary characters. They exist to support the male leads, but they rarely have any influence on the story. In The Funeral, however, Clara and Jean are central to the film's emotional and moral conflict. Their opinions and actions shape much of the film's tension, making them vital to the story.

In films like The Godfather or Scarface, women are often passive figures who either accept their husband's criminal lives or are too afraid to speak up. But in The Funeral, Ferrara breaks this mold. Clara and Jean are fully developed characters with their own struggles, opinions, and emotional journeys. They are not just there to serve the men—they have their own place in the story. This is especially clear in Clara's attempts to stop Chez from seeking revenge. Her role is not just as a wife but as a moral counterbalance to Chez's violence. She actively pushes back against the norms of the gangster world, offering an alternative to the cycle of violence.

Jean, while quieter, also challenges the traditional role of women in gangster films. Her emotional distance from Ray shows that she doesn't fully accept the life he's chosen. She doesn't actively oppose him like Clara does with Chez, but her quiet disapproval is a powerful statement. Jean represents the women who are caught in the middle, unable to change the men they love but refusing to fully embrace the life of crime.

How the Tempio Women Influence the Men

Though Clara and Jean don't hold the power to completely change the course of the story, they have a profound impact on how the men experience their grief and rage. Chez is constantly pulled between his love for Clara and his need for revenge. Clara's attempts to reason with him create moments of doubt, even if he ultimately follows through with his plans for violence. Her presence softens some of Chez's harder edges, showing the audience that there's more to him than just a gangster seeking blood. Clara humanizes Chez, even as he drifts further from her emotionally.

Jean's influence on Ray is more subtle. While Ray never openly acknowledges Jean's disapproval, it's clear that her emotional distance weighs on him. Ray is a cold and calculating character, but his interactions with Jean reveal that he understands the toll his choices take on her. In this way, Jean serves as a reminder of the emotional consequences of Ray's decisions. Her quiet sadness adds depth to Ray's character, making him more than just a ruthless killer.

Ultimately, in The Funeral, Abel Ferrara gives women a central role in a genre where they are usually sidelined. Clara and Jean Tempio are not just background figures—they are essential to the emotional and moral fabric of the story. Clara's strong voice and Jean's quiet disapproval both challenge the men's choices, offering alternatives to the cycle of violence that defines their lives. These women are not passive observers but active participants, shaping the way the story unfolds. Through Clara and Jean, Ferrara shows that the roles of women in gangster films can be much more than just supporting characters—they can be the heart and soul of the story.

The Funeral Cast – The Family Ensemble

Here's a select breakdown of characters and cast members in Abel Ferrara's The Funeral:

- Raimondo "Ray" Tempio (Christopher Walken): Ray, the eldest brother in the Tempio family, is a high-ranking member of the New York Mafia. He is a stoic, calculating figure whose authority and wisdom hold the family together, even as he grapples with personal tragedy and the weight of his criminal life.
- Chez Tempio (Chris Penn): Chez, the volatile middle brother, acts as the family's enforcer. His unpredictable nature and violent tendencies make him a dangerous yet integral part of

their operations. Chris Penn's portrayal brings depth to Chez's inner turmoil, showcasing his struggle with loyalty and rage.

- Johnny Tempio (Vincent Gallo): Johnny, the youngest Tempio brother, leads a quieter life as a factory worker. Unlike his older siblings, Johnny avoids direct involvement in organized crime, though his connection to the family's world inevitably draws him into its orbit.

- Gaspare Spogli (Benicio Del Toro): Gaspare is a shrewd and ruthless figure in the criminal underworld, using a blend of cunning and brutality to rise to power. His interactions with the Tempio family reveal the cold, calculated nature of those who thrive in their world.

- Clara Tempio (Isabella Rossellini): Clara, Chez's wife and the mother of their children, provides a stabilizing presence in the Tempio family. While supportive of her husband's role in their criminal empire, she is deeply concerned about the risks it poses to their family's safety. Clara's strength and compassion anchor the family during moments of crisis.

- Cesare (Paul Hipp): Cesare is loyal and dependable, but his recklessness often leads to significant consequences for himself and those around him.

- Rosario (Victor Argo): Rosario is a trusted associate of the Tempio family. Wise and pragmatic, he navigates the complex politics of the criminal underworld with care, offering valuable guidance to the Tempio brothers as they face mounting challenges.

- Jean (Annabella Sciorra): Jean, Ray's wife, is a devoted mother and a supportive partner. Though she stands by her husband, she is acutely aware of the dangers his criminal life brings to their family. Fiercely protective, Jean strives to shield her loved ones from the consequences of Ray's choices. These are the main characters and cast members in

The Funeral, each contributing to the film's rich and immersive portrayal of the Tempio family and their struggles in the criminal underworld of 1930s New York City.

Christopher Walken as Raimondo "Ray" Tempio

Christopher Walken, originally named Ronald Walken, was born on March 31, 1943. He is an acclaimed American actor, known for his extensive contributions to film, television, and stage. Walken has received numerous awards and nominations throughout his career, including an Academy Award, a BAFTA Award, and a Screen Actors Guild Award. He has also been nominated for two Primetime Emmy Awards and two Tony Awards. In 1963, Christopher Walken met Georgianne Thon during a tour of West Side Story. They got married in January 1969. However, the couple did not have any children. According to Walken himself in interviews, this factor played a significant role in allowing him to focus on his highly successful career.

Walken began his film career in supporting roles, making his feature film debut in Sidney Lumet's The Anderson Tapes (1971) alongside Sean Connery. He gained recognition for his performances in films such as Next Stop, Greenwich Village (1976), Roseland (1977), and Annie Hall (1977). However, it was his portrayal of the troubled Vietnam War veteran Nick Chevotarevich in The Deer Hunter (1978) that propelled him into the spotlight and earned him an Academy Award for Best Supporting Actor. He was later nominated for the same award for his role as con artist Frank Abagnale's father in Steven Spielberg's Catch Me If You Can (2002).

Since his breakthrough, Walken has appeared in a diverse range of films, both as a lead actor and in supporting roles. Some notable examples include The Dogs of War (1980), Brainstorm (1983), The Dead Zone (1983), A View to a Kill (1985), At Close Range (1986), Biloxi Blues (1988), King of New York (1990), The Comfort of Strangers (1990), Batman Returns (1992), True Romance (1993),

Pulp Fiction (1994), Suicide Kings (1997), Sleepy Hollow (1999), Man on Fire (2004), Wedding Crashers (2005), Hairspray (2007), Seven Psychopaths (2012), A Late Quartet (2012), and the first three films in the Prophecy series. He has also lent his voice to animated films such as Antz (1998) and The Jungle Book (2016).

Christopher Walken is a highly accomplished actor who has made significant contributions to the entertainment industry and has received widespread recognition for his exceptional talent.

Chris Penn as Cesarino "Chez" Tempio

Christopher Penn, born on October 10, 1965, and passing away on January 24, 2006, was a talented American actor. He was known for his roles as tough characters, often cast as villains, working-class thugs, or in comedic roles. Christopher Penn was the brother of famous actor Sean Penn and musician Michael Penn. He appeared in various noteworthy films, including The Wild Life (1984), Reservoir Dogs (1992), The Funeral (1996), Footloose (1984), Rush Hour (1998), Corky Romano (2001), True Romance (1993), Beethoven's 2nd (1993), Short Cuts (1993), The Boys Club (1996), All the Right Moves (1983), At Close Range (1986), Pale Rider (1985), and Starsky & Hutch (2004). His outstanding performance in The Funeral earned him the prestigious Volpi Cup for Best Actor at the 1996 Venice Film Festival.

Annabella Sciorra as Jean

Annabella Sciorra, who was born on March 29, 1960, is an American actress. She became famous for her debut film role in True Love (1989), for which she was nominated for an Independent Spirit Award for Best Female Lead. In the 1990s, she had a successful career in movies such as Spike Lee's Jungle Fever (1991), The Hand That Rocks the Cradle (1992), Abel Ferrara's The Addiction (1995), James Mangold's neo-noir crime drama Cop Land (1997), and What Dreams May Come (1998). Sciorra's performance as Gloria Trillo in The Sopranos (2001–2004) earned her an Emmy Award nomination, and she also played Det. Carolyn Barek in Law & Order: Criminal Intent (2005–2006). In addition to her work on screen, she has been praised for her stage performances, including winning a Theatre World Award for her role in The Motherfucker with the Hat on Broadway in 2011.

Isabella Rossellini as Clara Tempio

Born June 18, 1952, Isabella Rossellini is an Italian actress and model. She is famously known as the daughter of Swedish actress Ingrid Bergman and Italian film director Roberto Rossellini. Rossellini achieved great success as a Lancôme model and has had a thriving career in American cinema.

Her acting career took off after her breakthrough role in White Nights in 1985. She further gained recognition for her memorable performance in David Lynch's Blue Velvet in 1986, which earned her the Independent Spirit Award for Best Female Lead. Rossellini has appeared in numerous notable films such as Cousins (1989), Wild at Heart (1990), Death Becomes Her (1992), Fearless (1993), Wyatt Earp (1994), Big Night (1996), Roger Dodger (2002), Infamous (2006), Two Lovers (2008), Enemy (2013), Joy (2015), and La chimera (2023). In addition to her film career, she has also lent her voice to popular animated movies like Incredibles 2 (2018) and Marcel the Shell with Shoes On (2021). Rossellini will also be seen playing the role of General Malice in the TV series Human Resources in 2023.

Rossellini's talent has been recognized with several awards and nominations. She received a Golden Globe Award nomination for her role in the HBO film Crime of the Century (1996) and was nominated for a Primetime Emmy Award for Outstanding Guest Actress in a Drama Series for her performance in Chicago Hope (1997). She has also made guest appearances in popular sitcoms like Friends and 30 Rock, as well as dramas including Alias and The Blacklist. In 2022, she portrayed Simone Beck in the HBO series Julia.

Vincent Gallo as Giovanni "Johnny" Tempio

Vincent Gallo, born on April 11, 1961, is a multi-talented American, excelling in various fields such as acting, directing, writing, producing, music, and modeling. He has been recognized with numerous prestigious awards, including the Volpi Cup for Best Actor, and has received nominations for other esteemed honors such as the Palme d'Or, the Golden Lion, and the Bronze Horse.

In his earlier years, Gallo had an unconventional upbringing, with involvement in local mafia activities during his childhood. He initially pursued a career as a Formula II motorcycle racer before showcasing his skills as a painter and musician. He collaborated with renowned artists like Jean-Michel Basquiat and Lukas Haas. Eventually, Gallo shifted his focus to film and television, initially taking up minor roles in projects such as The Equalizer (1989) and Goodfellas (1990). However, he quickly rose to prominence as a lead actor in movies like Arizona Dream (1993), The House of the Spirits (1993), Palookaville (1995), The Funeral (1996), Stranded (2001), Tetro (2009), Metropia (2009), Essential Killing (2010), and The Legend of Kaspar Hauser (2012).

Gallo is equally skilled behind the camera and has directed, written, and starred in three independent films: Buffalo '66 (1998), The Brown Bunny (2003), and Promises Written in Water (2010).

Beyond his contributions to the arts, Gallo has explored his musical abilities by releasing solo albums on Warp Records in the early 2000s, He has ventured into modeling, collaborating with renowned fashion houses and brands such as Calvin Klein, H&M, Supreme, and Yves Saint Laurent by lending his striking presence to their campaigns and photoshoots.

Benicio del Toro as Gaspare Spoglia

Benicio del Toro, born on February 19, 1967, is an actor and producer who has received much praise and recognition for his work. He has been honored with an Academy Award, a BAFTA Award, a Golden Globe Award, two Screen Actors Guild Awards, and a Silver Bear for his memorable portrayal of police officer Javier Rodriguez in the film Traffic (2000), a character who is both disillusioned and morally upright.

Del Toro is mainly known for his breakthrough role as the eccentric and hard-to-understand criminal Fred Fenster in The Usual Suspects (1995). He also gained attention for his performances as Benny Dalmau in Basquiat (1996), earning consecutive Independent Spirit Awards for both films, as well as Dr. Gonzo in Fear and Loathing in Las Vegas (1998), gambling addict Franky "Four-Fingers" in Snatch (2000), and the menacing antagonist Jackie Boy in Sin City (2005).

His portrayal of revolutionary Che Guevara in Che (2008) garnered widespread acclaim, earning him the Best Actor award at both the Cannes Film Festival and the Goya Awards. Del Toro's role as Alejandro, a mysterious and ruthless agent on a mission to dismantle a drug cartel in Sicario (2015), also received critical acclaim and multiple award nominations, including a BAFTA nomination for Best Supporting Actor.

Del Toro has appeared as the Collector in the Marvel Cinematic Universe, drug lord Pablo Escobar in Escobar: Paradise Lost (2014), Lawrence Talbot in the 2010 remake of The Wolfman, and the codebreaker in Star Wars: The Last Jedi (2017). In 2018, he starred as Richard Matt in the Showtime miniseries Escape at Dannemora, receiving a Primetime Emmy Award nomination for Outstanding Lead Actor in a Limited Series or Movie.

Gretchen Mol as Helen

Gretchen Mol, an American actress and former model, was born November 8, 1972. She gained recognition for her role as Gillian Darmody in the HBO series Boardwalk Empire (2010–2014). Throughout her career, she has also appeared in notable films including The Funeral (1996), Donnie Brasco (1997), Celebrity (1998), Rounders (1998), Sweet and Lowdown (1999), The Thirteenth Floor (1999), 3:10 to Yuma (2007), and Manchester by the Sea (2016). Mol's portrayal of the protagonist in The Notorious Bettie Page (2005) earned her a nomination for the Satellite Award for Best Actress – Motion Picture Drama.

John Ventimiglia as Sali

John Ventimiglia is an actor from the United States. He is known for his role as Artie Bucco in the popular HBO series The Sopranos. He has had a recurring role as Dino Arbogast, the Chief of the Organized Crime Control Bureau for the NYPD, in the American police procedural/drama series Blue Bloods on CBS.

Paul Hipp as Ghouly

Paul Hipp was born July 16, 1963, an American actor, singer, songwriter, and filmmaker. Initially, he started his career by performing as a musician in various clubs. Paul began to gain recognition for his appearances in TV shows and commercials. Eventually, he debuted in the New York theater scene with the off-Broadway production of Rockabilly Road, performed at the West Bank Theater.

Hipp began a fruitful collaboration with Abel Ferrara that would span many years. He became an integral part of Ferrara's core group of actors, which included Christopher Walken, Harvey Keitel, and Willem Dafoe.

David Patrick Kelly as Michael Stein

David Patrick Kelly, born on January 23, 1951, is a multi-talented American actor, musician, and lyricist. Throughout his career, he has graced both the big and small screens, earning recognition for his performances in various films and television series. Kelly's most iconic role is that of the main antagonist, Luther, in the beloved cult film The Warriors (1979). He is also renowned for his collaborations with acclaimed director Spike Lee, featured in films such as Malcolm X (1992), Crooklyn (1994), and Chi-Raq (2015). Additionally, he has worked extensively with the visionary David Lynch, appearing in Wild at Heart (1990), the television series Twin Peaks (1990–91), and its revival in 2017.

Kelly's impressive work extends to other notable productions, including 48 Hrs. (1982), Commando (1985), The Crow (1994), The Funeral and Last Man Standing (both 1996), The Longest Yard (2005), Flags of Our Fathers (2006), where he portrayed President Harry S. Truman, and a recurring role in The Blacklist (2015).

Chapter 10

The Visual Style and Aesthetics in The Funeral

The Funeral is not just a film driven by dialogue or story; its visual style plays an essential role in building its atmosphere. Cinematographer Ken Kelsch's work alongside production design, costumes, and set choices contributes to the film's deep, brooding mood. Every visual detail feels intentional, reflecting the film's dark themes of death, grief, and revenge.

Ken Kelsch's Cinematography

Ken Kelsch, who has collaborated with Abel Ferrara on multiple projects, uses a distinctive visual language in The Funeral. The film's muted, often shadowy lighting creates a heavy, oppressive atmosphere, which mirrors the film's bleak narrative. The lighting is often dim, adding a somber tone that lingers throughout the film. Kelsch is masterful at capturing the emotional weight of scenes through the use of chiaroscuro lighting, where the contrast between light and dark symbolizes the characters' internal struggles.

Take, for example, the scenes that unfold during Johnny's funeral. The dark interiors, paired with flickering candlelight, create a sense of gloom and foreboding. The camera often lingers on characters' faces in these moments, highlighting their grief. Kelsch's use of close-ups, combined with low lighting, captures the pain etched on their faces. The shadows around them seem to swallow them up, symbolizing how grief and revenge are engulfing their lives.

Kelsch also uses wide shots that emphasize the empty spaces around the characters. These wide frames serve as visual representations of the emotional distance between the Tempio brothers, especially between Ray and Chez. This subtle visual storytelling helps reinforce the idea that, while they are bound by family ties, their emotional isolation from one another is profound.

The Use of Color in Conveying Themes

One of the striking elements of The Funeral is its limited color palette. The colors used in the film are often dark, muted, and earth-toned, which aligns with the film's themes of death and mourning. Blacks, greys, and browns dominate the scenes, giving the film a cold, desolate feeling. These colors not only reflect the bleakness of the characters' world but also highlight the inevitable descent into violence that drives the plot.

In some key moments, a sharp contrast of colors is used to draw attention. For example, in scenes where Johnny's coffin is shown, the red velvet inside the coffin stands out starkly against the dark surroundings. The red serves as a visual representation of the blood that has been shed and will be shed as the brothers seek vengeance. It is a subtle but effective way to remind the audience of the violent undercurrent that runs throughout the film.

The film also makes use of stark whites, particularly in the scenes set in the funeral home. The white sheets and walls of the funeral parlor stand in contrast to the dark clothing worn by the Tempio brothers. This use of white reinforces the theme of death while also suggesting a kind of cold sterility, a world where death is ever-present but devoid of emotion or warmth.

Set Design and Period-Specific Elements

The period-specific set design in The Funeral adds a layer of authenticity to the film, grounding it in the 1930s. From the dimly-lit, richly textured interiors of the Tempio family home to the smoky, crowded bars where the brothers meet, the production design evokes a sense of time and place that is crucial to the film's mood.

The family home, with its heavy wooden furniture, dark drapery, and religious icons, reflects the old-world values that the Tempio family clings to, even as they navigate the violent world of organized crime. The religious symbols are particularly striking, especially in scenes where characters struggle with moral questions about revenge and redemption. The constant presence of crucifixes and religious paintings in the background serves as a reminder of the spiritual weight that looms over their decisions.

Another standout location is the funeral parlor, which is designed to feel cold and detached, further emphasizing the theme of death. The sterile white walls, the polished wood of the coffin, and the lack of personal touches make the funeral feel almost clinical, as though death has become routine for the Tempio family. This coldness is contrasted with the raw emotion of the characters, creating a tension between the physical environment and their internal grief.

Costume Design and Character Identity

Costumes also play a significant role in establishing the film's tone and reflecting the characters' identities. The characters' wardrobe is deeply tied to their roles in the gangster world. The Tempio brothers are often seen in black or dark-colored suits, typical of the gangster genre, but with a sense of restraint that aligns with the film's introspective tone.

Ray, the eldest brother, is almost always dressed in a tailored black suit, which enhances his cold and calculated demeanor. The sharpness of his suits reflects his control and composure, but the dark color hints at the violence and corruption that lie beneath. Chez, on the other hand, has a more disheveled look, with his clothing often appearing slightly untidy. This reflects his more emotional and unstable nature, especially as he unravels throughout the film.

The women's costumes also play a critical role in shaping their characters. Clara, played by Isabella Rossellini, often wears simple, elegant dresses in muted tones, which reflect her quiet strength and moral clarity. Her wardrobe is understated, emphasizing her role as a stabilizing force in Chez's chaotic life. In contrast, Jean, Ray's wife, is dressed in slightly more glamorous outfits, which suggest her desire to distance herself emotionally from the violence that surrounds her.

Camera Angles and Scene Composition

One of the key elements of The Funeral's visual style is the careful use of camera angles and scene composition. Ferrara and Kelsch use a variety of angles to convey the emotional weight of scenes, particularly during moments of tension between the brothers.

In many of the more intense scenes, the camera is positioned at a low angle, looking up at the characters. This creates a sense of power and dominance, as though the characters are larger than life, driven by forces beyond their control. This technique is used particularly effectively in scenes with Ray, where his quiet intensity is magnified by the low-angle shots.

Close-up shots are also used sparingly but powerfully. When Ferrara does move in for a close-up, it's usually during moments of emotional vulnerability. For example, in a key scene where Chez breaks down, the camera lingers on his tear-streaked face, allowing the audience to fully feel the weight of his grief. The close-ups in The Funeral are not just about showing emotion—they are about forcing the audience to confront the characters' pain.

Lighting and Atmosphere

Lighting is used in The Funeral not just to create mood but to reflect the inner emotional states of the characters. The film is predominantly low-lit, with scenes often bathed in shadows. This darkness serves as a visual metaphor for the characters' moral struggles and the looming presence of death.

In some scenes, the lighting is almost completely natural, with the characters illuminated by flickering candlelight or dim lamps. This adds to the film's realistic, grounded feel, making the moments of emotional intensity feel raw and authentic. In other moments, the lighting is more stylized, with sharp contrasts between light and shadow. These moments often occur during the more violent or confrontational scenes, where the harsh lighting mirrors the characters' internal conflicts.

In conclusion, The Funeral is a film where every visual choice contributes to the overall mood and themes of the story. From Ken Kelsch's cinematography to the period-specific set design, costume choices, and use of color, every element works together to create a world steeped in death, grief, and the search for meaning in a violent world. The visual style of The Funeral is not just about aesthetics—it's about deepening the audience's understanding of the characters and the emotional weight they carry. Through these carefully crafted visuals, Ferrara and his team create a film that lingers in the mind long after the final frame.

Chapter 11

Once You Pull the Trigger, There's No Going Back

The Funeral is a film deeply rooted in the idea of irreversible actions, encapsulated by the notion that "Once you pull the trigger, there's no going back." In this chapter, we will explore how the choices of the characters, particularly those tied to violence and betrayal, set in motion a chain of events from which there is no escape. The film's focus on the consequences of these decisions serves as a grim reminder of the inevitability of downfall in the criminal underworld.

Irreversible Decisions in Key Scenes

One of the film's most poignant moments is the assassination of Johnny Tempio, the youngest of the three Tempio brothers. His murder is the catalyst that drives the entire plot of The Funeral. The family's grief, especially Chez's emotional breakdown and Ray's calculated desire for vengeance, underscores the gravity of Johnny's death. The act of pulling the trigger on Johnny sets off a series of violent retaliations that ultimately consume the Tempio family. The killers believe that the consequences of their actions can be contained, but the film shows us that such decisions have far-reaching effects, spinning beyond control.

Another significant scene occurs when Ray decides to exact revenge on the man responsible for Johnny's death. He coldly pulls the trigger, ending another life and deepening the cycle of violence. Ray's decision represents not just the end of his victim's life, but also the sealing of his own fate. Once he commits this act, Ray's downfall becomes inevitable. His choice to kill marks a point of no return, where redemption or peace is no longer attainable. The film doesn't just focus on the physical act of violence, but on the emotional and psychological weight that comes with such irreversible decisions.

Character Study: The Tempio Brothers and Their Choices

The three Tempio brothers—Ray, Chez, and Johnny—each represent different aspects of moral decay and the consequences of their criminal lifestyle. Johnny's carefree attitude towards life, coupled with his reckless involvement in crime, leads to his untimely death. His murder is a direct result of his decisions, emphasizing how even seemingly minor choices in the world of crime can lead to devastating consequences.

Ray, the eldest brother, is portrayed as a cold, calculating figure. His approach to violence is methodical, and he sees it as a necessary tool for maintaining power and control. But as the film progresses, Ray's choices bring him closer to his own moral and emotional collapse. His decision to seek revenge for Johnny's death is driven by a sense of familial duty, but it ultimately leads him down a path of destruction. Ray's actions highlight the film's central theme: once a violent act is committed, there's no way to undo it, and the consequences are inescapable.

Chez, the middle brother, represents the emotional core of the family. Unlike Ray, who is detached and calculated, Chez is overwhelmed by grief and guilt. His decisions are often impulsive, driven by his emotions rather than logic. Chez's inner turmoil is evident throughout the film, especially in the moments where he contemplates his own role in the family's downfall. His choice to confront his own demons through violence leads to his inevitable downfall. Chez's story arc serves as a cautionary tale about the dangers of letting emotions dictate one's decisions in the world of crime.

The Fall of Criminals: Case Studies from The Funeral

The fall of Johnny Tempio is perhaps the most striking example of how criminal actions lead to inevitable downfall. Johnny's murder is the direct result of his involvement in a dangerous world where loyalty and betrayal often collide. His death sets the stage for the other characters' downfalls, serving as a reminder that no one in the criminal underworld is safe from the consequences of their actions.

Ray's fall is equally tragic. His calculated, cold approach to violence initially gives him a sense of control, but as the film progresses, it becomes clear that he, too, is unable to escape the consequences of his choices. Ray's decision to avenge Johnny's death leads to a cycle of violence that ultimately consumes him. His fall from grace is gradual, marked by a slow unraveling of his composure and moral clarity. The film shows that even those who seem in control of their actions are still subject to the unrelenting consequences of their violent choices.

Chez's fall is perhaps the most emotionally charged. Unlike Ray, who tries to maintain a sense of control, Chez is consumed by guilt and grief. His decision to confront his own role in the family's downfall leads him to a point of no return. Chez's inability to cope with the emotional weight of his choices ultimately leads to his destruction. The film portrays Chez's fall as a direct result of his emotional vulnerability in a world that demands detachment and control.

The Consequences of Criminal Actions

The personal consequences of the characters' actions are profound. For Ray, his decision to seek revenge for Johnny's death leads to his emotional and psychological downfall. He becomes consumed by his desire for vengeance, losing sight of any chance for redemption or peace. Chez's emotional instability and impulsive decisions lead him to a similar fate. Both brothers, in their own ways, are trapped by their choices, unable to escape the consequences of their actions.

The societal consequences are equally significant. The world of The Funeral is one where violence begets violence, and the cycle of revenge is never-ending. The Tempio brothers' actions not only lead to their own downfalls but also contribute to the broader decay of the society they live in. The film presents a bleak picture of a world where crime and violence are met with more crime and violence, with no hope for resolution or redemption.

The line "Once you pull the trigger, there's no going back"[68] is not just a reflection of the characters' personal experiences but a broader critique of the criminal lifestyle. The film suggests that those who choose a life of crime are bound to face the consequences of their actions, whether they realize it or not. There is no escaping the inevitable downfall that comes with living in a world where violence and betrayal are commonplace.

Symbolism of Irreversible Actions

Throughout The Funeral, there are several symbols and motifs that reinforce the idea of irreversible actions. The gun, for example, is a constant presence in the film, serving as a symbol of violence and the finality of death. Once a character pulls the trigger, there is no undoing the act, and the consequences are set in motion. The gun becomes a metaphor for the choices the characters make, representing the point of no return.

The funeral itself serves as another powerful symbol. It is a reminder of the inescapability of death and the consequences of the characters' actions. The funeral scenes are somber and heavy, filled with a sense of finality. The characters are constantly confronted with the reality of death, both in their personal lives and in the world they inhabit. The film uses the funeral as a backdrop for its exploration of irreversible actions, reminding the audience that once a life is taken, there is no going back.

---

68 *The Funeral, Directed by Abel Ferrara (October Films; 1996).*

In conclusion, The Funeral is a powerful exploration of the consequences of violence and betrayal. Through its characters' irreversible decisions, the film illustrates the inevitable downfall that accompanies a life of crime. The line "Once you pull the trigger, there's no going back"[69] serves as a thematic anchor, reminding the audience that every action has consequences, and those consequences are often inescapable.

---

69 *The Funeral, Directed by Abel Ferrara (October Films;1996).*

Chapter 12

The Funeral: Critical Reception

Critic Reviews

"Ferrara and his writing partner Nicholas St. John, who also made "King of New York," "The Bad Lieutenant" and "The Addiction," are interested in deeper issues than mere revenge. (...) You're engaged on a moral level rarely found in movies about violence."- Desson Thomson: The Washington Post[70]

"The Funeral is about the kinds of gangsters the Corleone family might have become, if they had all gone to college (...) here is a gangster movie that does not want setups or payoffs like traditional gangster movies (...) Rating: *** (out of 4)."- Roger Ebert: rogerebert.com[71]

"Hot-blooded, broodingly well-acted new gangster film (...) [Ferrara] still finds sharp new ways to explore the nuances of a trite-sounding story." -Janet Maslin: The New York Times[72]

"In a film of strong performances, Penn's is the standout. He finds the madness in Chez that is the key to Ferrara's tale"- Peter Travers: Rolling Stone[73]

---

70 *https://www.washingtonpost.com/wp-srv/style/longterm/review96/funeralhowe.htm By Desson Howe Washington Post (November 08, 1996).*

71 *https://www.rogerebert.com/reviews/the-funeral-1996*

72 *https://www.nytimes.com/1996/11/01/movies/on-crime-and-conscience-among-brothers.html*

73 *https://www.rollingstone.com/tv-movies/tv-movie-reviews/the-funeral-101958/*

"Charles Lagola's resourceful production design, careful location work by lenser Ken Kelsch and tasteful period costumes by Mindy Eshelman contribute to an authentic sense of time and place." - Emanuel Levy: Variety[74]

"While The Funeral has the usual Ferrara touches — violence with sting, sex with kink — it's also his least typical work. Not since 1986, when he directed the pilot episode of the underrated TV series Crime Story, has Ferrara done a period piece, and if The Funeral inevitably lapses into *Godfather*-style grandiosity, it's also his most clearheaded, emotional movie to date."- Ken Tucker: Entertainment Weekly[75]

"Ferrara puts an interesting spin on the story by casting Annabella Sciorra and Isabella Rossellini as the two men's wives who attempt to throw in their two cents."- Jeffrey M. Anderson: Combustible Celluloid[76]

"A psychologically strung-out tale stuffed full of ideas and inspired moments."- Nick Schager: Lessons of Darkness[77]

"Film after film, Ferrara and St. John are finding new ways to scream." -Mick LaSalle: San Francisco Chronicle[78]

---

74 *https://variety.com/1996/film/reviews/the-funeral-1200446907/ By Emanuel Levy*

75 *https://ew.com/article/1996/11/22/movie-review-funeral/ By Ken Tucker Ken Tucker (November 22, 1996).*

76 *https://www.combustiblecelluloid.com/archive/funeral.shtml*

77 *https://www.nickschager.com/nsfp/2006/05/the_funeral_199.html*

78 *https://www.sfgate.com/movies/article/Buried-by-the-Mob-Chris-Penn-in-eerie-Funeral-2959589.php*

"Ferrara's eerie version of crime-wracked New York City of the 1930s." - Barbara Shulgasser: San Francisco Examiner[79]

"The performances in The Funeral are all electrifying. Ferrara also aligns himself with many of his longtime associates in the creation of The Funeral, most notably screenwriter Nicholas St. John, music composer Joe Delia, and cinematographer Ken Kelsch. Their contributions are intrinsic to what we think of as a "Ferrara" film."- Marjorie Baumgarten: Austin Chronicle[80]

---

79 *https://www.sfgate.com/news/article/crime-leads-to-a-funeral-3114224.php*

80 *https://www.austinchronicle.com/events/film/1997-11-22/the-funeral/* *By Marjorie Baumgarten, (Saturday, November. 22, 1997).*

Chapter 13

THE GREATEST GANGSTER MOVIE YOU'VE NEVER SEEN:

Abel Ferrara's The Funeral - Afterword
By Brad Stevens

" ... with him (Chris Penn) playing that, and knowing his history and knowing who he is - but he's an actor, he's an actor playing a role. And again, he's one of the reasons you're writing this book, because these people came together, Nicky and all the people you're talking about, we came together at the perfect time ". - Abel Ferrara to Danny Stewart

Abel Ferrara is perhaps the greatest artist currently active in cinema. This, clearly, is not a claim that would meet with general agreement. Indeed, for most 'with it' consumers of culture Ferrara is (depending upon which school of received opinion one subscribes to) either a clumsy exploitation hack or a has-been occasionally churning out half-conceived works designed to do little more than remind us that he is still alive. Yet Ferrara's *maudit* status, far from something which need be apologized for, is crucial to our understanding of his importance. In an era dominated by mindless franchises and blandly anonymous streaming product, serious filmmakers must be opposed, in every way conceivable, to dominant trends. For oppositional art of this kind to meet with marginalization, commercial failure, and critical disdain is thus not only predictable, but also inevitable and, in a certain sense, welcome. For what would succeeding mean in a world where that intelligent engagement with a popular audience for which classical Hollywood was notable recedes ever further with each passing year?

Those claims I am making for Ferrara might, then, seem as absurd as insisting, when their innovations had yet to be assimilated, that Vincent van Gogh was the finest painter of his generation, Stravinsky's The Rite of Spring a work of genius, Herman Melville's Moby Dick the Great American Novel. All these creators met with ridicule from 'experts' who regarded themselves as arbiters of contemporary taste. And it is my belief that Bad Lieutenant, Snake Eyes (aka Dangerous Game), The Blackout, New Rose Hotel, Mary and Padre Pio will eventually be seen in a similar light, their former rejection regarded as incomprehensible.

Which makes it all the more important that those attuned to the vibrations of Ferrara's genius not only encourage awareness of this *oeuvre*, but also do the research necessary, while those involved are still among the living, to establish precisely how such remarkable films came into existence. It is to this task that Danny Stewart has devoted himself, taking just one of the many gems directed by Ferrara - The Funeral - and subjecting it to intense critical analysis, meticulously situating it artistically, thematically, historically and commercially while conducting the kind of investigation which will not always be possible, interviewing the director and as many of his key collaborators as were willing to share their experiences.

And if the greatness of The Funeral, as with that of any masterpiece, still remains, must remain, ultimately inexplicable (even, one suspects, to its author), this is the inescapable result of approaching artistic creation not with a wish to be fashionable or admired, but rather with a need (for it has to be a need rather than a desire) to explore the complexities of human existence as honestly and thoroughly as possible. Those wishing to comprehend The Funeral are unlikely to come across a better guide than this vital contribution to Ferrara studies.

Film Credits

Directed by
Abel Ferrara

Screenplay by
Nicholas St. John ... (written by)

Produced by
Jay Cannold ... associate producer
Michael Chambers ... executive producer
Mary Kane ... Producer
Margot Lulick ... line producer (uncredited)
Patrick Panzarella ... executive producer
Randy Sabusawa ... co-producer (as Randall Sabusawa)
Annabella Sciorra ... associate producer
Russell Simmons ... associate producer

Music by
Joe Delia

Cinematography by
Ken Kelsch

Editing by
Mayin Lo
Bill Pankow
Jim Mol ... (uncredited)

Casting By
Ann Goulder

Production Design by
Charles M. Lagola

Art Direction by
Beth Curtis

Set Decoration by
Diane Lederman

Costume Design by
Melinda Eshelman

Makeup Department

Patricia Regan	...	makeup artist
Nancy Tong	...	hair stylist

Production Management

Jay Cannold	...	production supervisor
Mary Kane	...	production manager
Jasmine Kosovic	...	post-production supervisor (as Jasmine Kosovic')

Second Unit Director or Assistant Director

Laura Cercone Fiorino	...	second second assistant director (as Laura Cerone Fiorino)
Noga Isackson	...	first assistant director
Jenny Peek	...	dga trainee
Christopher Surgent	...	second assistant director (as Chris Surgent)

Art Department

Suzanne E. Cestare	...	second props master (as Suzanne Cestare)
Hallie Coletta	...	scenic artist

Hallie Coletto	...	Scenic
Frank DeCurtis	...	on-set dresser
Guido DeCurtis	...	lead man
Robert Dillon	...	key carpenter
Douglas Fecht	...	set dresser (as Doug Fecht)
Stephanie Ferrante	...	art department coordinator
David Greenhouse	...	scenic
Claude Horstmann	...	foreman
Mark Horstmann	...	construction coordinator
Ross Huttick	...	set dresser
Paul Loret	...	second construction grip
Christine Moosher	...	buyer
Ed Newins Jr.	...	key construction grip (as Edward Newins Jr.)
Stanley Pasay	...	camera scenic
Jon Ringbom	...	charge scenic
Amy Safhay	...	greens
Eric Stepper	...	prop master
Greg Sullivan	...	scenic
Harriet Zucker	...	prop shopper
Daniel Kimmel	...	art department production assistant (uncredited)

Sound Department

Patricia Brolsma	...	boom operator
Jason Canovas	...	dialogue editor
Rosa Howell-Thornhill	...	sound mixer
Kathleen King	...	boom operator
Karen McMullen	...	assistant sound editor (as Karen McMullen Homer)
Todd Miller	...	sound effects editor
Fred Rosenberg	...	dialogue editor
Greg Sheldon	...	supervising sound editor

Wyatt Sprague	...	sound apprentice
Jeffrey Stern	...	dialogue editor
Mel Zelniker	...	re-recording engineer: Sound One Corp. (as Mel J. Zelniker)

Special Effects by

| J.C. Brotherhood | ... | special effects supervisor |

Visual Effects by

| David Fuhrer | ... | video consultant (as David Furher) |

Stunts

| Phil Neilson | ... | stunt coordinator |
| Carl Paoli | ... | stunt double: Christopher Walken (uncredited) |

Camera and Electrical Department

Maria Calvaruso	...	second assistant camera
John Clifford	...	still photographer
Joseph Donohue	...	best boy grip (as Joseph G. Donohue III)
Andrea Dorman	...	first assistant camera
Steve Drellich	...	camera operator
Samuel G. Friedman	...	electrician (as Samuel Friedman)
Jim Galvin	...	electrician
Pedro Hernández	...	rigging grip (as Pedro Hernandez)
Eric M. Klein	...	grip (as Eric Klein)
Robert Kummert	...	key grip (as Rob Kummert)
John Paul McIntyre	...	dolly grip (as Jack McIntyre)
Charlie McNamara	...	gaffer (as Charles McNamara)
Linda Phillips	...	electrician
Larry Steinberg	...	grip
Jennifer Stuart	...	camera trainee

Phil Testa	...	best boy
Stephen Treadway	...	second assistant camera
Robert Vuolo	...	electrician (as Rob Vuolo)

Casting Department

| Sylvia Fay | ... | extras casting |

Costume and Wardrobe Department

Dorit Avnir	...	costume assistant
Joseph Cesarelli	...	additional wardrobe
Diane Collins	...	wardrobe assistant
John Corbo	...	set costumer
Beth Lincks	...	additional set costumer (as Beth Links)
Thomas Stokes	...	wardrobe supervisor (as Tom Stokes)
Ruthie Tanami	...	wardrobe assistant
Alana West	...	additional wardrobe

Editorial Department

Patricia Bowers	...	associate editor (as Trissy Bowers)
Suzanne Ceresko	...	post-production assistant
Pamela Chmiel	...	assistant editor (as Pam Chmiel)
Kenna Doeringer	...	first assistant editor
Jamal El-Amin	...	apprentice editor
Tony Grocki	...	assistant editor (as Anthony Grocki)
Marla Hanson	...	editor: video
Kent McGrew	...	color timer
Jim Mol	...	creative consultant: picture
Woody Richman	...	apprentice editor (as T. Woody Richman)
Nick Smith	...	apprentice editor
Greg Speed	...	second assistant editor
Robin Whittaker	...	post-production intern (as Robin Quinn)

Laura Franses	...	location assistant
Kathy Gatto	...	location intern (as Kathy Grissom)
Sebastian Hoschirl	...	location intern
Jonathan Manzo	...	assistant location manager
Michael Nickodem	...	location manager
Natile Orango	...	location intern
Dan Solomon	...	location intern
Joseph Stephans	...	location assistant
Matt Whitcher	...	location assistant

Michael Burrelle	...	musician: The Chez Lounge Band
Joe Delia	...	musician: The Chez Lounge Band (as 'Killer' Joe Delia)
James Flatto	...	music editor (as Jim Flatto)
Jill Meyers	...	music consultant
Jim Mol	...	creative consultant: music
Jon Sigel	...	musician: The Chez Lounge Band (as Jonathon Sigel)
Ron Thomas	...	musician: The Chez Lounge Band

| Karen Kelsall | ... | script supervisor |
| Daniel Kimmel | ... | script intern |

David Babcock	...	driver (as David Jay Babcock)
Ryan Boyd	...	Driver
Irv Gooch	...	picture vehicles (as Ira Gouch)
Dennis Kelly	...	Driver
Robert James Rauer	...	driver (as Robert Rauer)
Louis Volpe	...	transportation captain (as Lou 'Sonny' Volpe)

| Karen Barber | ... | assistant to director |
| Donna L. Bascom | ... | legal counsel (as Donna L. Bascom Esq.) |

Leonard John Bruno	...	production placement (as Leonard Bruno) / promotions (as Leonard Bruno)
James 'Morris' Byrnes	...	set production assistant
Jim Carden	...	assistant accountant
Maya Churi	...	assistant to director
Juliet D'Annibale	...	assistant production coordinator
Lori Eastside	...	Choreographer
Kevin Greene	...	production accountant
Charles Houston	...	parking assistant
Jay Julien	...	legal counsel (as Jay Julien Esq.)
Carl Kelsch	...	office production intern
Kevin Kolovich	...	office production assistant
Gianluca Lazzaroni	...	production assistant
Mary Lugo	...	unit publicist: Clein & White
Eric Mathis	...	International Sales Agent: brazil
John Paul McIntyre	...	Cre ative consultant (as Jack McIntyre)
Frank McKenna	...	craft service: Meals On Reels (as Frank)
Michael McKenna	...	craft service: Meals On Reels (as Mike McKenna)
Mary Jackson Miller	...	assistant to producer (as Mary Jackson)
Pernilla Nelson	...	office production intern
Olivia Pi-Sunyer	...	production coordinator
Douglas Plasse	...	set production assistant (as Doug Plasse)
Roger Rawlings	...	office production assistant
Lynn Reich	...	set production assistant
Holly S. Rymon	...	assistant accountant (as Holly Rymon)
Jean-Andre Sassine	...	parking coordinator (as Jean Sassine)

John Shaw	...	set production assistant
Eric Shonz	...	insurance broker: Great Northern/ Reiff & Associates
Dena Silberstein	...	production placement / promotions
Richard Suffern	...	office production assistant
Teresita Tan	...	assistant accountant (as Teresita P. Tan)
Dave Brown	...	hat maker (uncredited)
Javier López de Ayala	...	Publicist: Spain (uncredited)
Judy Sharinger	...	legal delivery supervisor (uncredited)
Rick Washburn	...	weapons coordinator (uncredited)

Endnotes

i   *By Ilya Mauter - Own work, CC BY-SA 4.0, https://commons. wikimedia.org/w/index.php?curid=66975937*

ii   *By Georges Biard, CC BY-SA 3.0, https://commons. wikimedia.org/w/index.php?curid=59768282*

iii   *By This is a film envisioned by and directed by Abel Ferrara. - This is a The Driller Killer screenshot taken from the Internet Archive version at around the 1:26 mark., Public Domain, https://commons.wikimedia.org/w/index.php?curid=26140250*

iv   *By This is a film envisioned by and directed by Abel Ferrara. - This is a The Driller Killer screenshot taken from the Internet Archive version., Public Domain, https://commons. wikimedia.org/w/index.php?curid=26158327*

v   *By Lascher - Public Domain, https://commons.wikimedia. org/w/index.php?curid=28977039*

vi   *By Georges Biard, CC BY-SA 3.0, https://commons. wikimedia.org/w/index.php?curid=40754665*

vii   *By newspaper press photo, Rome, Italy - Book: Notorious, by Donald Spoto, Public Domain, https://commons. wikimedia.org/w/index.php?curid=14857064*

viii   *By MGM - http://images.moviepostershop.com/dr-jekyll-and-mr-hyde-movie-poster-1941-1020524819.jpg, Public Domain, https://commons.wikimedia.org/w/index.php?curid=104722629*

ix   *By Metro-Goldwyn-Mayer - https://movieposters.ha.com/ itm/horror/dr-jekyll-and-mr-hyde-mgm-1941-lobby-card-11-x-14-horror/a/58124-54112.s, Public Domain, https:// commons.wikimedia.org/w/index.php?curid=88783836*

x   *By MGM - source, Public Domain, https://commons. wikimedia.org/w/index.php?curid=59189123*

xi   *By RKO Radio Pictures - Public Domain, https://commons. wikimedia.org/w/index.php?curid=95114090*

xii   *By Trailer screenshot - Casablanca trailer, Public Domain, https://commons.wikimedia.org/w/index.php?curid= 1757126*

xiii   *By Bill Gold - https://www.hometheaterseattle.com/ Casablanca-1942-Movie-Poster_p_160.html,   Public Domain,   https://commons.wikimedia.org/w/index.php? curid=25315862*

xiv   *By MGM photographer - Public Domain, https://commons. wikimedia.org/w/index.php?curid=20029748*

xv   *By "Copyright 1944 Loew's Incorporated". - Scan via Heritage Auctions. Cropped from original image., Public Domain,   https://commons.wikimedia.org/w/index.php? curid=89341257*

xvi   *By "Copyright 1946 RKO Radio Pictures Inc." - Scan via Heritage Auctions. Cropped from the original image., Public Domain,   https://commons.wikimedia.org/w/index. php?curid=87339746*

xvii   *By RKO Radio Pictures (corporate author), The Kobal Collection. Photographer: Ernest Bachrach. - Chicago-Sun Times, Public Domain, https://commons.wikimedia.org/w/ index.php?curid=9571484*

xviii   *By RKO Radio Pictures - Photoplay, 1946, Public Domain, https://commons.wikimedia.org/w/index.php?curid= 74511266*

xix   *By RKO Radio Pictures - Public Domain, https://commons. wikimedia.org/w/index.php?curid=74650633*

xx   *By Fox Film Corporation - https://assets.mubi.com/images/ notebook/post_images/18752/images-w1400.jpg,   Public Domain,   https://commons.wikimedia.org/w/index.php? curid=61174978*

xxi   *Printed by M. R. Litho Co. in New York, per the credit seen on the bottom-left corner. - Scan via Heritage Auctions.,*

Public Domain, https://commons.wikimedia.org/w/index. php?curid=85716109

xxii *By Astor Pictures Corp. - IMDb, Public Domain, https:// commons.wikimedia.org/w/index.php?curid=75942680*

xxiii *By author - Vieira, Mark A. (2019). Forbidden Hollywood: The Pre-Code Era (1930-1934): When Sin Ruled the Movies (eBook). New York: Running Press. Hachette Book Group. ISBN 978-076-246-675-7., Public Domain, https://commons. wikimedia.org/w/index.php?curid=113729859*

xxiv *By Warner Bros. - Sourcearchive, Public Domain, https:// commons.wikimedia.org/w/index.php?curid=86245021*

xxv *Distributed by First National Pictures. - Scan via Doctor Macro's High-Quality Movie Scans. Retouched to reduce noise and more closely match the brightness/coloration seen on lower-res scans like those at, e.g., MoviePosterShop. See unretouched original below in upload history., Public Domain, https://commons.wikimedia.org/w/index.php? curid=86985125*

xxvi *Distributed by First National Pictures. - Scan via Heritage Auctions. Cropped from the original image., Public Domain, https://commons.wikimedia.org/w/index.php?curid= 86985433*

xxvii *By Warner Bros. Pictures Inc. - The Movie Database (TMDb), Public Domain, https://commons.wikimedia.org/w/ index.php?curid=73997940*

xxviii *By Trailer screenshot - The Petrified Forest trailer, Public Domain, https://commons.wikimedia.org/w/index.php? curid=2217186*

xxix *By Street & Smith; photograph by Vandamm Studio - Picture Play, June 1935 (pp. 34–35) immediate source Note that the final uploaded version is of higher quality than that shown in the magazine scan., Public Domain, https://commons. wikimedia.org/w/index.php?curid=68729457*

xxx   *Motion Picture Production Code (Hays Code), cover of a paper copy.- web, Public Domain, https://commons.wikimedia.org/w/index.php?curid=29507708*

xxxi   *By Whitey Schafer - https://thefilmstage.com/wp-content/uploads/2013/03/hayscode.jpg, Public Domain, https://commons.wikimedia.org/w/index.php?curid=112093165*

xxxii   *By Producers Releasing Corporation - source, Public Domain, https://commons.wikimedia.org/w/index.php?curid=57424140*

xxxiii   *By Distributed by United Artists. - Scan via Heritage Auctions. Cropped from the original image., Public Domain, https://commons.wikimedia.org/w/index.php?curid=86896980*

xxxiv   *By Distributed by United Artists. - Scan via Heritage Auctions. Cropped from the original image and lightly retouched; see upload history for unretouched original., Public Domain, https://commons.wikimedia.org/w/index.php?curid=86896988*

xxxv   *By Employee(s) of Allied Artists - http://mymovies.444px.com/t/p/w1280/rpdzQDD325a1tx4eOeLF2CuItmk.jpg, Public Domain, https://commons.wikimedia.org/w/index.php?curid=18511380*

xxxvi   *By Allied Artists - Heritage Auctions, Public Domain, https://commons.wikimedia.org/w/index.php?curid=86985755*

xxxvii   *By Reynold Brown - http://i.imgur.com/5nPSk.jpg, Public Domain, https://commons.wikimedia.org/w/index.php?curid=24767766*

xxxviii   *By Warner Bros.-Seven Arts - Brownwood Bulletin, Public Domain, https://commons.wikimedia.org/w/index.php?curid=131339561*

xxxix   *By Distributed by Warner Bros.-Seven Arts. - Scan via Heritage Auctions. Cropped from the original image., Public Domain, https://commons.wikimedia.org/w/index.php?curid=92403294*

xl   *By NBC - RMY Auctions, Public Domain, https://commons. wikimedia.org/w/index.php?curid=51017796*

xli   *By Published by Culture Publications, Public Domain, https://commons.wikimedia.org/w/index.php?curid= 69990398*

xlii   *By (RKO Pictures) - Public Domain, https://commons. wikimedia.org/w/index.php?curid=28390937*

Index

Numbers in **bold** indicate photographs

About the Author

Danny Stewart has authored the book, "Solder: From Script to Screen," which features interviews with numerous cast and crew members of the 1998 science fiction western film. He is dedicated to preserving the passion for cinema and has also contributed to the documentaries "Brothers in Arms," which explores the Academy Award-winning film "Platoon," and "Cleanin' Up the Town: Remembering Ghostbusters," which he executive produced.